Business in the 21st Century

A South African CEO Perspective

THANDIWE GAMA, PhD

Business in the 21ˢᵗ Century: A South African CEO Perspective
Copyright © 2019 Thandiwe Gama

First printing, 2019

ISBNS:
978-0-620-85549-5 (Amazon KDP e-book)
978-0-620-85533-4 (Amazon KDP paperback)

Published by Thandiwe Gama, PhD
Johannesburg, South Africa
Email: tgama@mweb.co.za
Twitter: @DrThandiwe
Linkedin: Dr Thandiwe Gama

Editing and layout: Russel Brownlee
Cover design: Tallulah Lucy

DEDICATION

THE INSPIRATION towards accomplishing my PhD could not be fully appreciated without briefly knowing the story behind it, because it feels like my entire life was in preparation for this achievement.

I grew up under the care of my paternal grandmother who valued education, but had not attained any because she was orphaned by the time she was a toddler! She grew up and got married as a teenager and was gifted two boys (one of whom is my father). Sadly, they also lost *their* father when the eldest was hardly five years old, and their mother was just in her early twenties! I spent my time daring the universe to be kind to me – to provide me with an opportunity to obtain the highest academic levels, not only for myself but also for my grandmother, even beyond her grave: This one is for you, Ziya!

Having grown up as the eldest in our big family, this became a consuming passion, as well as a dare to my younger siblings that the sky is indeed the limit! As the first one in the race, the baton was firmly in my hand.

I remain grateful to my family and friends, whose love carried me through the upheavals of academic life. My father offered me the financial vehicle I needed to propel me through my education. My daughter's love and willingness to sacrifice quality time with her mom provided the driving force for me to see this journey through.

My siblings' support, encouragement and assistance were invaluable – particularly Nomcebo, who spent sleepless nights searching for relevant references.

I am deeply appreciative to my professor (Prof. Koos Uys) for his academic and intellectual support and guidance.

My work colleagues generously accepted my request to take on some of my work, and sometimes assisted with editing, typing, and searching for material at various libraries. I would also like to acknowledge my professional editor, Laura Durham, for her proofreading and attending to language issues. Throughout this journey I was blessed to ride with truly remarkable souls.

CONTENTS

FOREWORD

Prof. Frans Cilliers (UNISA)

IN THIS BOOK, Thandiwe Gama acknowledges her loved ones and family background as some of the most important inspirational factors contributing to her exceptional passion and drive towards completing her PhD in Industrial Psychology. Her work as encapsulated in this book, reflects her diligence, perseverance, performance motivation and role modelling for those around her.

Although the book's text is based on her doctorate degree research findings, one never gets the sense of reading an academic thesis. Her translation of the material into a user-friendly manuscript is highly commendable. She shows an endearing capacity to formulate her ideas to her audience – organisational leaders and management as well as everyone interested in the challenges associated with the world of work. This she does without compromising the seriousness and gravitas of the topic, its constructs and meaning.

Her qualitative research design and the standard of the empirical work give the book a solid academic grounding and offers the reader a high level of face validity and trustworthiness in reading about and implementing new thinking, ideas and guidelines towards containing the anxiety in our present and future work roles.

The key findings of the research are very well presented and can be summarised as follows. The present South African business and leadership scenario is extremely challenging, complex and paradoxical as experienced by prominent CEOs. They stress the necessity of sustainability in an unpredictable environment. This includes the reparation of broken relationships as a result of our legacy. Hope is placed on the implementation of the National Development Plan (NDP) as an endeavour to stimulate the economy and, through this, the quality of life for all South Africans.

Thandiwe firmly believes and gives convincing evidence that management thinking influences organisational vision, mission and culture, as well as how and what decisions are made, and how these aspects manifest in effective business performance. The contribution of the research can be framed as an understanding of current mental models in business as a point of departure towards shaping the economic, social, political and technological fibre of our country.

To write about the 21st-century world of work is not easy. So much is speculated about what the future holds, what the demands are that organisations will be confronted with and how organisational leaders will have to prepare themselves to cope with the uncertainty and the new reality. This book represents a sensitive exploration through the eyes of present Chief Executive Officers as a sample of leaders grounded in the present as well as with an expectation and vision of the future of their businesses.

In Chapter 1, as introduction, she provides a historical view on the development, role and relatedness between paradigms, world views and mental models as the driving forces towards coping with complexity and securing success and sustainability in the 21st-century business.

Chapter 2 applies the above in the South African business context with insight about how the dynamics of complexity, diversity and ambiguity manifests in our unique socio-political situation. She argues about the challenges of South Africa as a new democracy, and SA as a global competitor, coping with 21st-century challenges. She affirms the relevance of the National Development Plan and is concerned about the present disconnect between government and business.

Her work gains face validity in Chapter 3, where she gives verbatim voice to her sample of business leaders. Her analysis of the themes is interestingly linked to task – e.g. leadership with a global outlook focussing on knowledge management and solutions for complex problems and technological advancement, as well as linked to people aspects – e.g. authentic leaders focussing on the development of the youth, the customer and social networks. She expresses a concern about the lack of a clear voice and impact within the business fraternity. Her research can be seen as a brave effort to make this voice heard.

Chapter 4 contains the integration of the empirical findings into two models. The first links social responsibility, the NDP and sustainability, and the second explicates sustainability achievement. She uses these models to provide a very insightful future perspective on business, organisational design and business culture for the 21st century.

In Chapter 5, Dr Gama bravely sets out the implications of the research findings for leaders in the 21st century. She does this beyond the already known jargon (such as volatility and unpredictability). Her shares her views on a much more complex behavioural level with reference to working in paradoxical positions in a systemic context – leadership of self, the other and the organisation. Indeed, Dr Gama, the time of framing the work as 'the business of business is business' is over.

I salute Dr Gama with the insight and bravery to say what we need to hear in an honest and open manner based on solid research – and not in service of what the politically correct audience wants to hear in order to repeat the past.

INTRODUCTION

Mzansi, what are you seeing in this dawn of the 21ˢᵗ century?

THE DAWN of the 21ˢᵗ century has ushered in a voice which speaks in a language that many are still grappling to comprehend – a language full of innuendos. It has dropped onto our world a plethora of new realities: Globalization, volatility of markets, uncertainty, ever-increasing speed – all of which characterize the VUCA (volatile, uncertain, complex, ambiguous) world. Yes, we need to listen and truly hear the message – the call for change and a whole new way of thinking!

And what of South Africa – what informs the thinking in this country dancing to a 21st-century song? Are you hearing your own thoughts? Are you following your thought processes? Are you measuring your steps as you brace into this new dawn? What lenses are you wearing as you attempt to look across the horizon and into the new day that is unfolding? Can you risk looking away or will you step boldly into the unknown?

Indeed, times have changed even for you Mzansi! Given the lingering challenges, the remnants of the old apartheid era that you are still grappling with, how are you negotiating your way through the global networks that await your wisdom, your riches, and your footprints? How will you make yourself known as a force to be reckoned with on the emerging global stages, that increasingly reveal themselves as the dawn dissipates?

Some thought leaders assert that these global stages require a new paradigm, one that can assist you in rising to the challenges of the 21st century. The entire globe is hearing the whispers relating to climate change and global warming. Technological advancement is at a gallop. The millennial world of work is requiring a re-think in terms of leadership. There is a need for ever-faster turnaround time of product or service delivery. Demands are being made for seamless access to information. We have expanding opportunities for management of new knowledge around the clock.

Wow! Mzansi, can you cope economically, socially, politically and technologically?

Politicians have coined a new term *Thuma mina*.

Socialists are calling for a new social fibre and social cohesion.

Economists have new measures for global currencies and formulas of demand and supply.

Technologists ask vigorous questions such as:

- Who's in your WhatsApp group, and what are they saying?
- What's your Twitter handle, and what are you tweeting?
- Who's in your Facebook page, and what are you posting?

Are the millennials in your organisations ahead of you Mzansi? They seem to be in tune with the new thinking. Scholars are saying you need a new leadership DNA because organisational DNA has changed. This now asks how nimble are you, how global are you, and how organic are your processes, systems, and policies?

The dawn of this new era is going to demand sustainability and this dawn will indeed be calling the shots!

None of us can wish away the paradigm of these emerging times, for to do so would run the risk of never witnessing the sunshine of our success in the 21st century and experiencing its warmth and comfort.

PhD Study

This book will share the findings of a study that was embarked upon to scientifically examine the current mental models operating in South Africa and their implications to business thinking in the context of the 21st century.

My interest in this was motivated by my own experience of having worked for many years within the overall area of Organisational Development, having studied organisational psychology and asked myself many questions relating to the theoretical and practical implications of these, particularly in this era of turbulence.

The reality is that the business fraternity, along with Labour and the Government, remains a very significant and influential pillar in the economy of our country of South Africa. Certainly, whatever mental models drive business thinking; these will be embedded in the relations that exist across these three spheres.

Also addressed in this book are some recommendations as to how a workable framework could be created to guide the strategic thinking of organisational leadership as it deals with the inevitable 21st-century issues of ambiguity, speed and complexity. The issue of sustainability is simultaneously rearing its head and calling for renewed thinking, adding yet another level of complexity for organisations in general. The suggested framework acts as a focusing lens onto these emergent realities and the call for sustainability management.

Executive Summary of The PhD Study

In order to make substantial sense of the management thinking within a particular business context at a particular time period, we have to identify the underlying mental models that drive such thinking.

Orientation and Research Purpose

Even though many theories in organisational leadership and management exist, the study of mental models within business remains an area hungry for further research. Mental models not only give meaning to the environment but also function as a frame of reference for action and interpretation of the social world in which we live. The PhD study that forms the basis of this book was to explore the mental models of South African industry leaders (CEOs) as they lead within the 21st century.

Motivation of the Study

Business is faced with increased challenges in order to thrive, or even just survive in these uncertain times. Exploring mental models could assist in establishing where business is currently positioned and what drives leadership thinking.

Research Design, Approach, and Method

The approach adopted involved conducting intensive qualitative interviews with seven CEOs of different business sectors within South Africa, as well as one member of the Planning Commission in the Presidency. It also included an extensive literature review.

Key Findings

Business leaders considered the current times as challenging. Speed, complexity and paradox have become the norm. Sustainability has become the fundamental principle. Respondents acknowledged that sustainability has become the ruling paradigm. Due to the new reality and challenges faced, however, the focus has moved away from sustainability to dealing with complexity and unpredictability. Within South Africa, the challenge is exacerbated by the poor relations between business, government and labour, given the apartheid legacy. Leaders I spoke to were calling for better relations, especially in light of the implementation of the National Development Plan (NDP), which was considered vital in shaping our economy.

Contributions/value-add

This study envisaged bringing forth the voice of business regarding their challenges and investigating their opinions of the road ahead for South Africa. By better understanding the current mental models in business, we can understand leaders' actions and reactions to our social landscape. Mental models and management thinking in the business fraternity, in general, is a phenomenon of interest when it comes to shaping the economic, social, political and even technological fibre of any economy at any particular time. This is so because, without any doubt, in any economy, business forms an integral part of its social, political, and economic character. Thus the role and significance of mental models in shaping management thinking continues to be a core principle in any economy around the globe. Management thinking drives the manner in which business is conducted, including the vision and mission of the organisation, decisions made, its priorities and performance as well as its culture.

When we speak of management thinking, we need to consider the underlying mental models. Such a topic easily lends itself to in-depth scrutiny of what drives prevalent management thinking. While some may have a vested interest in theoretical, philosophical or scholastic purposes, the truth of the matter is that for anyone to make sense of the management thinking within a particular business context at a particular time period, the underlying mental models need to be understood.

Structure of this Book

The structure of this book is set out with a deliberate intent to highlight, firstly, the relevance of the field of Industrial and Organisational Psychology in guiding the thinking, approaches and strategies of organisations both in current times, as well for the envisaged future. One cannot argue against the fact that any business/organisation always has a purpose, mission, and vision for its current life or for its existence well into the foreseeable future.

Secondly, the intent was to establish the thinking that drives business now and what the outlook is for the future as we mature into the 21st century and as South Africa establishes itself within the global world.

Using the principles of coaching, we create meaning through:

- Establishing who and where we are currently, what makes or has made us who we are, and what informs our outlook of where we want to be if the end picture can be drawn. If it cannot, then how do we navigate through the journey of life in a meaningful way?
- Considering how we make sense of the world we are currently in, and what informs this sense.
- Finally, determining how we carve our path to our envisaged future and what meaning we can derive from the experience.

We often find it easier to articulate things that we *don't* want for ourselves, rather than what we do. Even after eliminating all that is *not* wanted, we may still need to define precisely what we desire and where we would like to see ourselves. The essence of this book is an attempt to encourage business to create a picture of an ideal organisation within a 21st century South African economy. This is dependent on identifying the operating paradigms and the mental models that could facilitate the thinking required.

Moving from these fundamental principles of coaching, the book is structured as follows:

Chapter 1 focuses on what we know about the evolution of management and leadership, as guided by the challenges at hand. It thereby builds a case for what seems to be the order of the times, the Sustainable Management Organisation.

Chapter 2 addresses the circumstances in South Africa, and also provides the context for the economy of South Africa with the dawn of the new era of sustainability. As depicted in Figure 1 below —on one hand we have the paradigm of sustainable management, and on the other, we have the economy with its layered challenges. These serve to define our current positioning within the global world.

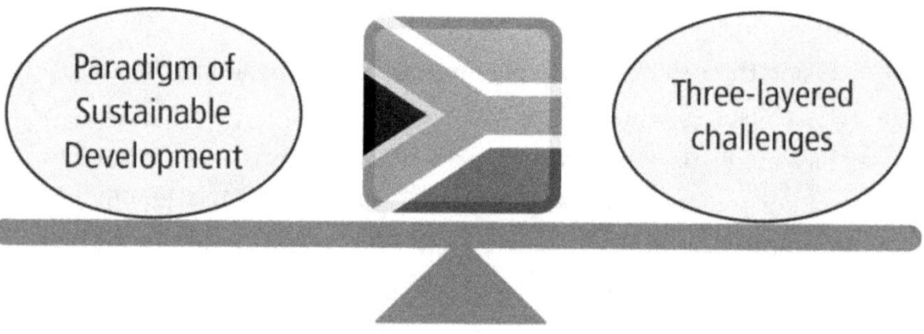

Figure 1 Current circumstances in South Africa

Sense is then made of this, using the principles of coaching, to establish how businesses can adopt relevant thinking models, forge ahead and position themselves to thrive in the 21st century.

Chapter 3 addresses these mental models.

Chapter 4 discusses sense-making of the themes and mental models.

The last two chapters consolidate these mental models. A framework of the business of the 21st century and its implications for business in South Africa is discussed. This framework could guide businesses in general, even global organisations, as they strive to remain relevant in the 21st century.

1

THE CHANGING NATURE OF BUSINESS AND THE UNDERLYINGMANAGEMENT PARADIGMS

UNDENIABLY, times have changed and will continue to do so, ever more rapidly. What worked yesterday no longer finds relevance in turbulent times.

In a business sense, this has certainly been accompanied by the need for a change in management thinking, theories, and practices. By understanding the evolution of management theories, we can better understand the movement from previous mental models to what is more current.

Management Thinking Evolution: Theoretical Background

We need to acknowledge the massive transformational thinking within business fraternities across the globe from the 19th to the 21st century.

The First Evolutionary Change

We can consider the first evolutionary change as the emergence of management of work and task in its own right.

In a1988 *Harvard Business Review* article, scholar Peter Drucker took us back to the turn of the 19th century when two major evolutions in the concept and structure of organisations became evident within a very brief period of not more than two to three decades.[1] This development firstly commenced in Germany, when Georg Siemens, the founder and head of Germany's premier bank, Deutsche Bank, saved the electrical machinery company his cousin Werner had founded after Werner's sons and heirs had mismanaged it to a point of almost total collapse. By threatening to cut off the bank's loans, he forced his cousins to handover the company's management over to professionals. At the same time, the massive restructurings of the US railroads and industries by JP Morgan, Andrew Carnegie, and John Rockefeller, resulted in more or less comparable undertakings where the management of work showed favourable outcomes.

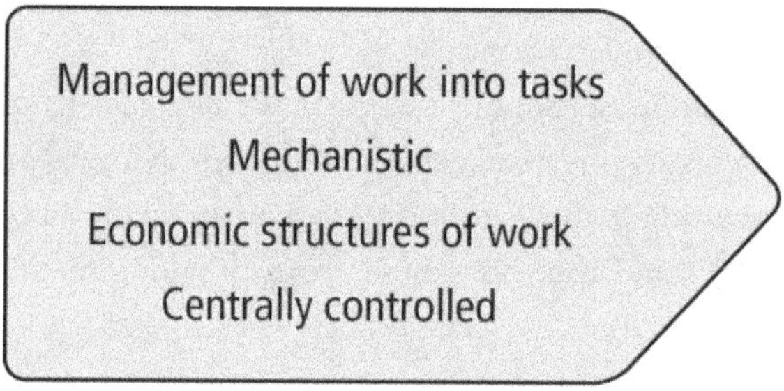

Figure 2: The Management of Work Paradigm

Something not mentioned in Drucker's article, but relevant, was Taylor's work on the principles of scientific management around 1900, which emphasised three specific issues. First, the recognition that business organisations were specialised social entities different from other social and economic structures. Second, the conception of organisations as mechanistic in nature – recognising that organisations were rational and deterministic and were to be understood by their goals and their strategies for getting there by fitting human and physical components (organisation structure) together. Third, the inclusion of the physical sciences in organisational functioning.

The conception of the organisation as a centrally controlled, mechanistic, rational entity has, however, been challenged since Taylor's conception.[2]

The Second Evolutionary Change

The second evolutionary change took place 20 years later with what was seen as the emergence of the modern corporation, with Pierre S du Pont restructuring his family's company in the US in the early twenties. This more or less coincided with Alfred P Sloan's redesign of General Motors a few years later and can be seen as the emergence of the Command and Control Organisation (CCO).In this stage of emergence of the organisation, emphasis was placed on decentralisation, central service staff, personnel management, the whole apparatus of budgets and controls, and the important distinction between policy and operations. A noteworthy development in this stage was the massive reorganisation of General Electric in the second half of the 20th century, an action that perfected the model most big businesses around the world (including Japanese businesses) followed at that stage.[3]

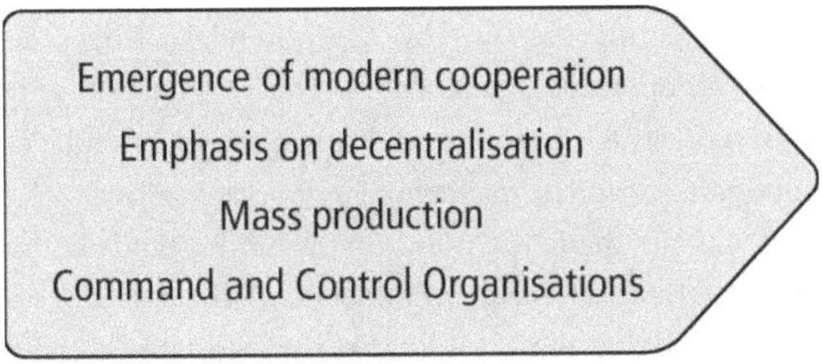

Figure 3: Command and Control Paradigm

Drucker envisioned a third period of change in which there would be a move away from CCOs to the organisation of department and divisions, and to the information-based organisation, the organisation of knowledge specialists. Drucker's assertion is that we can indeed perceive, albeit very dimly, what this organisation will probably look like. And we can identify some of its main characteristics and the central problems of its values, structure and behaviour. However, the actual job of building the information-based organisation is still ahead of us.[4]

Other scholars who expanded on Drucker's overview referred to this as the *first management reset*, the occurrence and combination of the rational principles of bureaucracy – the only management framework available – with the scalable technology of mass production. They referred to this as the emergence of the so-called Command and Control Organisation (CCO).[5]Anchored by the certainty of demand growth, the ability of CCOs to meet customer demand fostered an era of unprecedented economic growth. This is largely also a confirmation of Drucker's conception of this type of organisation.

What was referred to as the *second management reset* got triggered by a growing complexity of work, the rising education level of the workforce and innovations in management practice. This led to the creation of organisations committed to employee involvement, focusing on people as sources of creativity and innovation. They were not regarded as mindless beings requiring autocratic supervision to contribute but had the potential to become a key source of competitive advantage. These High Involvement Organisations (HIOs), however, did not necessarily replace CCOs as the dominant means of managing large organisations.

These scholars made the point that to understand the future of management, you first have to understand the past. "We cannot successfully build the nimble future-orientated, and socially savvy organisation of tomorrow if we do not understand why new management approaches are created."[6]

They presented three arguments as to why these concepts are no longer applicable.

The *first argument* was based on the assumption that in a CCO or HIO context, the business environment would be relatively stable, so incremental change would be feasible. With today's and tomorrow's worlds, the unpredictable, rapidly fluctuating and often chaotic external environment would demand rapid responses.

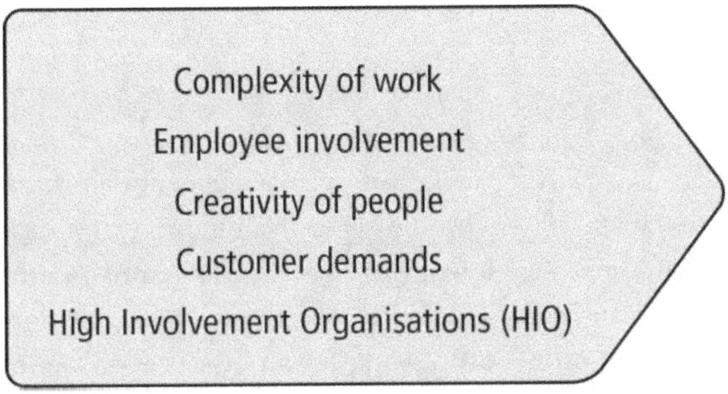

Figure 4: Complexity of Work Paradigm

Similarly, in the *second argument,* the business models and management principles of CCOs and HIOs were developed in an environment where there was more need for a strategic focus and for internal planning and organisation than for what would be required in an emergent global business context of the future. In the rapidly changing environment of the 21st century, unpredictability has become the new norm.

The *third argument* as to why the business principles and guidelines of the previous management era are not applicable any more is due to environmental degradation. It is occurring at an ever-increasing rate. The more material wealth organisations create, the more the natural environment suffers. They also stated that as long as management/organisations are not going to be held answerable for the damage caused to the environment, they would continue to destroy it.

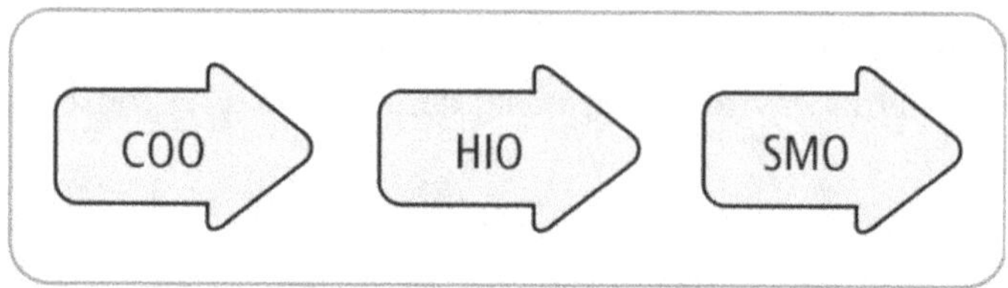

Figure 5: Sustainability Paradigm of value creation

There is a strong case for a management approach that recognizes that value creation is as significant as shareholder returns, without solely looking at shareholder returns as the only business indicator of success. Put differently, value creation must be judged using proper accounting for an organisation's impact on the planet and people as well as its profits. Two well-known management scholars, Lawler and Worley, chose the sustainable management organisation (SMO)as the name for this management reset.[7] The reset entails designing and sustainably managing effective organisations that suit today's *and* tomorrow's world. They strongly argue that the failure of the existing management approaches to address the major challenges the world is facing today necessitates a *third management reset*. In other words, it is about a new coherent approach to managing large complex organisations that fits today's and tomorrow's world. SMOs are regarded as more responsive and able to react more quickly and appropriately than HIOs.

These scholars go further to suggest two dimensions on which to judge organisational effectiveness in the context of sustainability:

1. Does the organisation *generate sustainable outcomes* and *act responsibly* toward all stakeholders? This is often referred to as the triple bottom line, but the broader principle is manifest in day-to-day decisions that give social and environmental outcomes. SMOs are designed to do consistently well in all three of these areas; they do not let the desire for profit squeeze out the other aspects.

2.   Can the organisation *sustain effectiveness*? This translates into questions about adaptability, innovation, risk management, and appropriate identity. SMOs assume little will be stable in the long-term. To be truly sustainable, SMOs commit not only to triple bottom line goals but also to having execution, innovation, and implementation capabilities that support change.

Core Principles and Practices of SMO Management

Four core issues determine the way of managing organisations. To be effective, SMOs must address each of them with principles and practices that fit the business environment and produce sustainable effectiveness. The following represents short descriptions of each of them:

1. The Way to Create Value

SMOs substitute robust strategies for competitive ones. A robust strategy is successful over a broad range of conditions over a long period and is capable of being amended to address short-term opportunities and threats when necessary. It is crafted to create a combination of social, environmental, and economic value. It looks for a series of momentary competitive advantages.

2. The Way to Organise Work

SMOs need a design that makes them adaptable, responsive to changing conditions, and responsive to multiple stakeholders. The structure, work processes, and management processes of SMOs need to facilitate innovation and execution, collaboration, and efficiency. Achieving this requires high levels of contact between employees and the business environment, the development of innovative units, flexible, budget-less control systems, new ways of working, and value-creating networks.

3.The Way to Treat People

Key to the success of organisations that create value based on their competencies and capabilities is how they treat talent. It is critical to attract, retain, develop, and motivate the right talent. To do this, SMOs need reward systems that focus on skills, talent-management systems that identify and retain the right employees, and performance management systems tied to the organisation's strategy.

4.The Way to Guide Behaviour

The combination of their organisation's leadership style and culture strongly influences how employees behave. An approach that creates leaders throughout the organisation and that rejects the imperial CEO model should guide SMOs. They need a culture that loves change, innovation, and sustainable performance.

In a quest to highlight the fundamentals of SMOs, another renowned scholar, Dr Jopie Coetzee, in his book *The Social Contract with Business: Beyond the Quest for Global Sustainability*, presents two world scenarios:[8]

- 'A world of inclusive globalisation' (WOIG) – a world scenario based on two powerful global forces, namely the need to improve human security and the need to eradicate systemic poverty through responsible business models.
- 'A world of destructive globalisation' (WODC) – an opposite scenario of destructive globalisation, argued from business models of reduced human security and increased poverty.

Based on his research and reasoning, Coetzee concluded that there is a clear sense that humanity has given its business, societal, and political leaders the mandate to lead humanity away from today's world of destructive globalization to a world of inclusive globalization; a mandate that requires a dual perspective to focus simultaneously on increasing humanity's broad security and eliminating systemic poverty. This duality in humanity's global sustainability mandate relates to the essence of today's business leadership dilemmas:

- the kind of economic delivery system that can deliver on both success criteria;
- the role, responsibility, and purpose of business leadership in society;
- the end purpose of a firm's vision, business models, and corporate social responsibilities; and
- the balance between the local and the global, the short and the long term.

Having briefly outlined the different perspectives and arguments of several reputable scholars in management and the apparent evolution of the modern organization, including the dimensions for judging organizational effectiveness and the evolutionary thinking of SMOs in the 21st century, let us delve more deeply into the thinking behind SMOs and emerging paradigms.

Organisational Evolutions – Emerging Paradigms

Given the complexities and speed of change in modern life, the analogy of sustainability seems set to replace traditional views of both leadership and the workplace. There is no doubt that the emerging modern organisation seems to call for management for sustainable effectiveness. The shift from the Industrial to the Information Age has already clearly transformed the workplace and the nature of work. Technology has placed much greater emphasis on data, swiftness and ongoing adaptation.

Around 2009, Tom Peters pioneered the concept of Chaos Theory where he presupposed a world far more complex than Newton's physics could explain, full of unintended and counterintuitive consequences.[9]In such a world, we cannot easily map the future because of its unpredictability and our inability to control it.

Judging from past developments and current models in organisational theories, today's organisations are still steeped in the need for managing turbulence, complexity and unpredictability. The new thinking is that times have once again changed, so alternative paradigms are required. Indeed, my research has also led me to believe that success for the emergent modern organisation will depend on appropriate leadership to create sustainable effectiveness, i.e. business sustainability. The world is full of unintended and counterintuitive consequences and often, in such a world, we cannot draw the map of the future in advance because we cannot predict the future or control it.[10]The world has become chaotic and complex. Building from Tom Peters' Chaos Theory, Tetenbaum's view is that complexity and paradox are factors that contribute to the chaos, and he asks very critical questions: What can we understand about Chaos Theory and its spin-offs, as well as its relevance to the complexity that characterises the world we live in now? And, is Chaos the new and emerging paradigm?

Business Sustainability as the Emerging Paradigm of the 21st Century

To date, most business leaders and management schools still operate under the delusion that the prevailing traditional business model based on economic rationalisation is unquestionable. Furthermore, the delusion that the prevailing business wisdom and models are still relevant continues to be held by some business leaders.

Others are, however, beginning to question this assumption and ask us to face the new reality head-on. Today it cannot be denied that the new business world is filled with changes and we can see this by the massive failures of the existing management approaches which deal with today's challenges through applying the traditional orthodoxies. The unspoken truth is that we cannot continue to conduct business as usual because sustainability will unavoidably be the central theme of this century, as economic growth was in the last century. Despite this being the current scenario in many countries, one challenge is that there are evidently some who still perceive the concept of a sustaining organisation as an impossibility. Put differently, not everyone views a sustainable organisation as a viable possibility, nor is the concept of sustainability fully intellectually defined or accepted. Maybe those who are not yet fully receptive need to realise that this new thinking does not imply that business profits will suffer compared with those in the last century of economic growth. Scholar Jon Marques maintains that, to the contrary, the gratification that will be earned from applying this mindset reaches far beyond financial profits, because it involves "doing good while doing well" in today's global environment.[11]This perspective views the economics of business as complementary to societal issues and the biosphere.

Further, Lawler and Worley propose the concept of value creation. Value creation is the capacity to generate maximum profits while creating value for humanity (people and planet), thereby according equal standing to social and environmental and economic priorities. These authors propose that organisations are now entering a third reset, where organisations/businesses should focus on a different kind of sustainability – that which refer to the "ability of an organisation to sustain itself in a tumultuous world."[12]

Evident common themes include:

- Firstly, organisations will no longer be able to function effectively on outdated perspectives and the need for different management thinking (another reset) is becoming evident.
- Secondly, the drive for profit, often even at the expense of the human, societal and environmental context within which a business operates, has become – or is becoming – obsolete and unsustainable.

- Thirdly, business can and needs to remain profitable while it is extending itself to the concerns of environmental sustainability.

However, although business sustainability is being broadly discussed on both a macro level (environmental sustainability) and a micro level (business viability and profitability), my study revealed that even though the concept of sustainability is being appreciated and mentioned, business leaders are still largely clinging to traditional orthodoxies influenced purely by economic rationalisation. This still typifies the strategic and economic discussions in many boardrooms, despite the complexities of the new era.

The message that stands out appears to be that the future organisation is still evolving, and while we may realise that previous approaches are no longer relevant, we should acknowledge that the job of building the organisation of the future will likely be a difficult one. But the time has come to work towards it because the centre cannot hold, so to speak. The 21st century seems to have come with increased complexity and change.

Characteristics of a Sustainable Organisation

Sustainable organisations engage in activities that contribute mainly in four ways.[13] They:

1. extend the socially useful life of organisations
2. enrich the planet's ability to maintain and renew the biosphere and protect all living species
3. enhance society's ability to maintain itself and to solve its major problems, and
4. maintain a decent level of welfare for present and future generations of humanity.

Some of the distinctive characteristics of a sustainable organisation would be:

- Replacing an emphasis on meeting shareholder expectations by an emphasis on meeting stakeholder expectations.

- Developing a new social and ecological contract that respects the rights of employees, the community, and the biosphere. This involves consulting stakeholders and securing their ongoing support for the organisation's right to operate.
- Corporate accountability to stakeholders, including future generations. This involves eliminating externalities such as waste and pollution.
- A new definition of wealth as increased and shared community value.
- A corporate culture of stewardship, involving the efficient and effective use of human and natural resources, and caring by contributing in a variety of ways to supporting a community that develops and enlarges human talent.
- Abandoning the short-term exploitation of people and the natural world and developing an active commitment to health, renewal, and regeneration.

In reference to Coetzee's concepts of the world of inclusive globalisation (WOIG) and the world of destructive globalisation (WODG), we see that organisations where sustainability is prized have the ability to hold a duality in thinking, being able to respond to the need to improve human security while eradicating poverty through responsible business models. In WODG organisations, on the other hand, human security is reduced and poverty is increased.

These two worldviews or scenarios highlight the progressive thinking carried through the WOIG which, to me, illustrates the thinking required in our country to eradicate the remnants of apartheid and to prize social responsibility.

Although, as mentioned, the concept of sustainable management is still often missing from organisational agendas, some business leaders in my study acknowledged that it was gaining their attention. These questions are indicative of the thinking that is beginning to occupy the minds of business leaders.

Is it important for business leaders to have a conscience and not just look at profits but also at sustaining and ploughing back into society?

South Africa is still catching up to the rest of First World thinking. In addition, in our unique circumstances, resources need to be channelled towards meeting the challenges created as we dismantle the apartheid legacy. However, the seed of sustainability thinking seems to be there. This seed needs be to be nurtured as the 21st century unfolds. If we are to indeed become a force to be reckoned with in the global world, and on the African continent, we certainly need to accelerate the catching up process.

Given the characteristics of sustainable organisations, some that have truly embraced these have delivered highly rated outcomes.[14] And yet, there have been some unintended consequences, such as global warming, large-scale pollution, destruction of ecosystems and species, and exploitation of the poor.

This question also remains: how can we create and support sustainable organisations that typify what is positive, but without harmful consequences?

Thus far, the following has been determined:

- There are unique developments in managerial mindsets/mental models.
- There are paradigm shifts in organisational evolution.
- There is a very real impact on business of external and environmental changes.

In conclusion, based on research as well as scholarly inputs and reasoning, there appears to be a common theme emerging throughout the globe that humanity has given its business, societal, and political leaders the mandate to lead humanity away from today's world of destructive globalisation towards a new era of inclusive globalization. This mandate requires a dual perspective, that is to focus on increasing humanity's broad security and eliminating systemic poverty, whilst concurrently aiming for appropriate business profits. This sustainability goal speaks to the core of today's business leadership dilemmas.[15]

Mental Models as Emergent from the Paradigms

Paradigms are considered applicable on a macro level, for example, as a science, or as an entire worldview. When the focus is on individuals or on personal concerns or perspectives, the term used is "mental models", as popularised by Senge in 2006. My own diagrammatic of the correlation is shown in Figure 6.

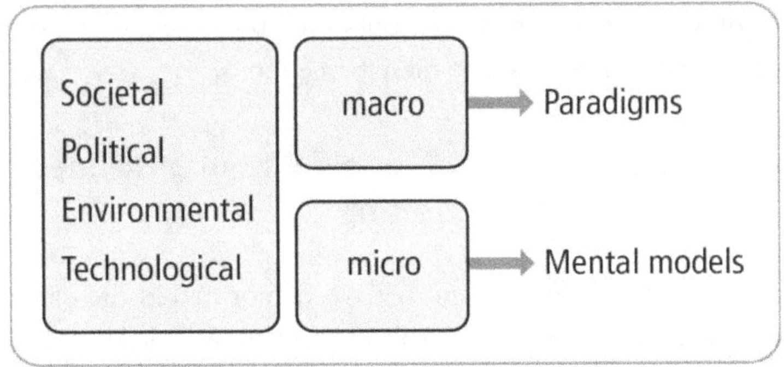

Figure 6: Relational understanding of paradigms and mental models

My study explored mental models in a business context as they relate to a paradigm with three levels – that is our unique situation as a country, the reality of globalization and the challenges presented by the 21st century. To create appropriate understanding, I will elaborate on my understanding of these mental models.

The concept of mental models has been in existence for a long time. Although previously referred to by psychologists as *schema/schemata,* the generally accepted term is now mental models. While there have been a number of definitions offered by theorists in the interdisciplinary fields of human/machine interaction, cognitive science, psychology, and organisational learning, the cognitive theorists[16] who have elaborated on this term seem to concur that mental models are the images, assumptions, and stories, which encompass every aspect of the world around us. These mental maps enable us to navigate the complex environments of our world.[17] In my reading on this subject, one writer describes these as *small-scale models* of how the world works constructed in our minds.[18] Senge and Kim support the view that these mental models, stemming from our own assumptions and beliefs about the world, have the capacity to affect what we perceive or "see" and thus influence how we act and react.[19]

My personal perspective, as used in my study, is simply that we are a product of our own perceptions of the external world and that our mental models shape these perceptions.

Relevance of Mental Models Within a Business Setting

Research studies in organisations have demonstrated the value of eliciting mental models in order to understand how leaders behave when responding to changes and disasters.[20] Therefore, I first determined the current mental models of those leaders with whom I spoke and then derived the themes that became apparent. By exploring their mental models, I could inquire into the thought patterns and reasoning of the business leaders in my study as they began to lead their businesses into the 21st century and grappled with sustainability.

My rationale was based on my appreciation that previous studies had found evidence to support the assertion that mental models affect strategic decisions and choices. Put simply, the value of a strategy depends on management's ability to effectively evaluate its business environment. This, of course, becomes especially critical in highly complex situations. Furthermore, when the relevance of mental models in business complexity was examined, it was discovered that mental models were the product of organisational learning mechanisms, such as active information gathering and information elaboration, as well as information dissemination, storage, and retrieval.[21]Where organisations used learning mechanisms and shared knowledge more intensively, there was higher congruence among members' mental models, and the change messages were more strongly embedded throughout the enterprise.

Conclusion

In conclusion, we have seen from the brief outline of existing literature and philosophical thinking that paradigms are associated with a world view and with contexts within which we operate, be it socially, politically, technologically and economically. Paradigms shape our individual mental models. Similarly, within business, these mental models become a basis for driving our business endeavours in time and space. The relevance here is that by revealing the mental models shaping leaders' interpretations of their current operating environment, we can understand and predict the influence these mental models will have on their perspectives and therefore, based on their views, whether a business is likely to succeed within this 21st-century context.

2

UNDERSTANDING BUSINESS IN SOUTH AFRICA

Part 1: The General Business Context

SINCE THE INCEPTION of democracy, South Africa has undergone extensive changes that have put the country in the public eye. The collapse of apartheid and the peaceful manner in which the country transitioned into a democracy still remains a miracle to many and has rendered South Africa an icon.[22]

The country's move away from race-related policies and practices into democracy has included holding successful national elections as well as local polls since the birth of the new democratic dispensation in 1994.Even though our transition narrative is applauded, the country still faces the challenges of eradicating the legacy and traces of apartheid. The collapse of the apartheid regime and the avoidance of a prolonged racial bloodbath was one of the major success stories of the late twentieth century. However, economic and social problems remain overwhelming. An extraordinary diversity typifies the social landscape, and although the country achieved a peaceful transition, there is much that still remains problematic and volatile. Generally, it is fair to say that much has been done to eradicate the racial laws of apartheid, but a lot still needs to be done.

The present government faces a daunting task – one of not only effectively entrenching a culture of democracy in its policies and practices as a country but also of playing a constructive role in Southern Africa and being part of the African continent and the world at large. In the last decade or so, the country has witnessed a sharp rise in protests by communities, as well as industrial unrest due to the inequalities that nevertheless remain in places of work, particularly the mines. South Africa has seen this decade marked by a culture of worker strikes and service delivery protests. Whilst the massacre at Marikana is certainly unprecedented in South African history since democracy, the rebellious behaviour characterising many demonstrations and service delivery protests is an indication that the country is still grappling with apartheid legacies. Housing, sanitation, electricity, water, and even discriminatory practices in workplaces in relation to income linger as spectres of the past. Numerous researchers have concluded that the pressing challenges of unemployment, poverty, service delivery, and inequality in the education system must still be addressed.[23]Dr Pundy Pillay, an established researcher, noted that South Africa was advancing into the 21st century grappling with six key socio-economic challenges:

- macro-economic policy
- the labour market
- poverty and inequality
- the social sector
- globalisation and the South African economy, and
- fiscal decentralisation.

He concludes that there is an interrelationship between these six challenges. Policymakers, therefore, need to recognise this linkage and cautiously and consensually consider how policy can be developed to tackle the pressing need to drastically reduce unemployment, poverty and inequality. The present government is undoubtedly facing a major task. They must not only deal with festering problems thanks to the previous dispensation and effectively entrench a culture of democracy but also play a value-adding role in Southern Africa.

At a regional African level, South Africa appears to be interested in integration and in playing a role in the African continent, such as the Southern African Development Community (SADC) and the African Union (AU). At an international level, the government has begun meaningful participation in international forums (such as the United National General Assembly), including overarching issues such as climate change, global financial and economic issues, the reform of international institutions, peace and stability in the Middle East, as well as relations within Southern African countries. For example, South Africa has witnessed the appointment of former deputy president Dr Phumzile Mlambo-Ngcuka to the UN and former health minister Dr Nkosazana Dlamini-Zuma to the AU.

On the government front, drastic political changes have brought about the need for implementing new policies to support South Africa's new dispensation. Government departments are having to increase capacity and productivity, with structural and, to a larger extent, attitudinal changes. Given the current reality that South Africa faces, the 21st century poses even greater challenges for those who manage the economic and political fields.

Attitudes and Mindsets in South African Business

Having outlined some key points in the journey towards full transformation, the question becomes, how does the South African context and its realities impact the thinking of business, given the broader challenges economically, socially, technologically, and politically?

Given the situation as described above, the business environment is continuously growing in complexity, diversity, and ambiguity. My perception is that since business finds itself unavoidably caught up in a social and political maelstrom, the emergence of the 21ˢᵗ century poses even greater difficulties, particularly from an economic perspective. Tough decisions will need to be made within the business community.

It appears that the 21ˢᵗ century is heralding changing contexts for business operation on a global scale. The country has entered an age where issues of globalisation, competition, speed, technology, and knowledge acquisition are changing the business platform. The global business world has not only increased in complexity but is also full of paradoxical and conflicting choices for business leaders. Uncertainty and ambiguity have become the norm. Business philosophers suggest that these anomalies may be calling for a new type of business with new thinking and new possibilities. This may indicate the emergence of a new paradigm emerging or simply an extension of the dimensions of the existing paradigm, where business and commerce are required to review traditional models and view business science through new lenses.

Top executives and industry leaders are beginning to face decisions that will not only impact the shorter-term value of their businesses, but also their economic, and social sustainability well into the future. A healthy balance between the myriad of issues and opportunities will require tough decision-making. For South African leaders, the dawning 21ˢᵗ century will certainly complicate matters, both in terms of their place within the country and as an inseparable part of the African continent.

South Africa's challenges seem to be occurring at three levels:

1. establishment of its critical and powerful role within the African continent
2. its role as part of the international global economy
3. its new democracy, and entrenchment of the culture thereof.

It can be argued, therefore, that business in South Africa is characterized by the reality of a three-layered challenge:

Firstly, business leadership is still wrestling with levelling the playing field across race and gender – in particular where black people and women were not part of the core economic streams. In South Africa, some individuals have asserted that the period between 1984 and 1994 erased the old concept of *business operating within the boundaries of business*, and, instead, offered a medium for political change.[24]Perhaps the truth in such a perspective can be substantiated through my own experience (around that period) of having witnessed business becoming fertile ground for the masses to push for further political developments, including organised labour strikes demanding equal pay for equal work, for affirmative action policies that were indeed effective, and for previously disadvantaged groups to be included in the economic mainstream. To date, we are inundated with stories of racial tensions, not only in business but also in private spaces. Burning issues of race and gender are a cancer that continues to eat away hard-won democracy and comes at the huge expense of effective progress, especially within the business sector.

On a second level, there are implications for big business, including its attempt to penetrate the global market and to operate within a free market system. As a result, competition has become tighter and more complex, and previous game plans and tactics are no longer adequate to ensure future success. In addition, South Africa is now participating on global platforms, for example, the African Union and the European Summit. This implies that South African business must be accepted as fit to compete at this level. Globally, leadership challenges are so immense that they seem to be calling for a different calibre of leader: that is, one who is capable of dealing with inconceivable convolution stimulated by the boundless pace of change.

On a third level, it is accepted that while the country as a whole, and specifically businesspeople, are still combating the plethora of issues emanating from both the first and second levels, a third layer of challenges has been introduced as the 21st century dawns. The third level was brought along by the emergence of the 21st-century era with its unique challenges of speed and heightened complexity in all aspects of our world. This has a vital pulsing dynamic of its own that creates an imperative for the revolutionization of the business world. These three levels of challenge must be dealt with simultaneously and certainly feature in boardroom discussions as leaders strive to steer their organisations towards their vision of success.

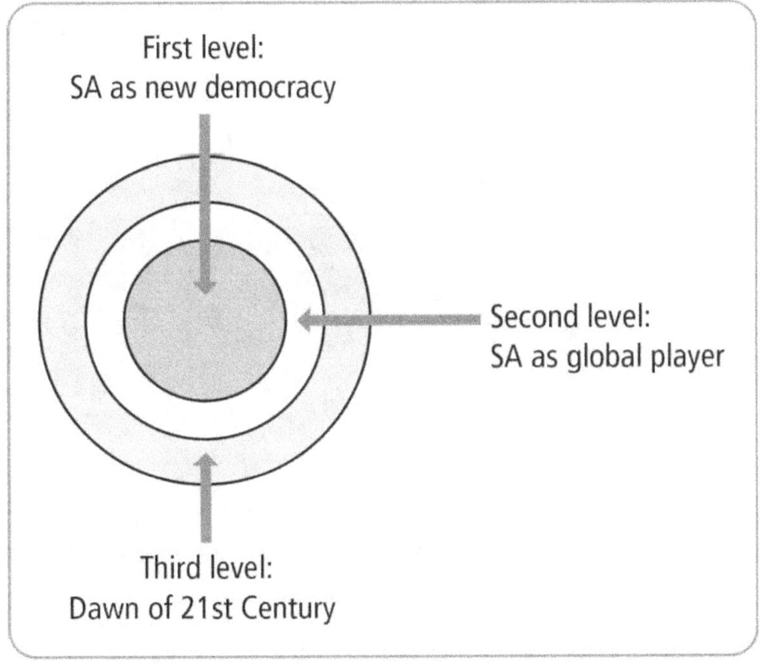

Figure 7: The three levels of challenge for business in South Africa

Conclusion

I believe the key features of the current South African business context centre around the following:

23

- The unique requirements of our new democracy as it relates to the business fraternity and the future challenges it presents.
- Operation on a truly global platform.
- The emergence of a profusion of challenges becoming evident in the dawning of the 21st century

Further, it is my belief that business leaders have the responsibility to ensure their businesses are enabled to thrive and, moreover, become sustainable in the 21st century and even beyond.

Part 2: South African Business in Relation to Government and Organised labour

In discussing leadership dynamics within a South African historical context, we cannot avoid exploring the nature of the relationship between industry leaders and those in government. It is no secret that this relationship has been and is still, largely, riddled with suspicion and misunderstanding on both sides. During my interviews, the launch of the NDP emerged as being a core component for enhancement of these relationships.

The launch of the NDP was mentioned by the business leaders I spoke to when they expressed their concerns about the future of South Africa. This inevitably formed a point of discussion and focus as they voiced their perspectives as to the extent to which the remnants of the apartheid legacy required their attention as they endeavoured to strategize and lead their organisations into a sustainable future.

I also conducted interviews with the Head of the Planning Commission to obtain their views about the future of the plan in relation to business as well as to South Africans at large.

National Development Plan: Business Sentiments

Some of the actual sentiments expressed include the following:

- "History of fundamental distrust between SA corporate sector and government: Discussions that ought to be taking place between government and business chambers are not taking place – we only have two or three business chambers, e.g. BUSA. Dysfunctional relationship is an inhibiting factor resulting in poor legislation, policy, and regulatory environment."
- "There is a very big disconnect between business and government."

- "This lack of effective dialogue between business and government affects us domestically but also affects us in all our offshore activities and how well we can actually compete globally."
- "Increase the level of trust between government and business so that we can deal with some of our issues that confront us as the country."
- "The biggest issue that has to be addressed is the lack of trust issue. I think we have thought as a country and also as a business and government that trust can just develop spontaneously. We need to do a lot more to build the trust, to understand that our fortunes are very tied at the hip. In other words, if government does not succeed, there is no way we, as business, can sustain the success we have. And likewise, without successful business, government must understand that it cannot succeed as well. This has not really happened."
- "In business, interestingly, we have to find a way of mending relations, building trust and learning to work together, because when you go out there you hear business saying there is almost no relationship between government and business, and if it exists, it's antagonistic. But that is talking in sort-of broad terms and talking about organised formations, because these complaints we hear when you talk to people, whether they are in BUSA (Business Unity of South Africa) and so on. They don't feel that connection."

Study participants (both from business and government) acknowledged that, historically, relations were riddled with mistrust and tension. Similar concerns were raised in the blueprint by the broader Business Leadership South Africa (BLSA) constituents:

"The collective BLSA identified the issue of trust and cooperation between government, labour, and business as

the major constraints to the successful implementation of
the NDP in this country."

"Remarkably, the BLSA was bold to admit that this trust-
less relationship has been raised in various forums over the
past two decades; it is not resolved, but nonetheless BLSA
acknowledge that both parties need to do more to rebuild
the bridge that connects them."

This clearly distant relationship between two significant role
players in the economy of the country – government and business
leadership – is recognisedas being a criticalchallenge to overcome if
the country's economy is to improve. As generally accepted, in the
post-apartheid dispensation the country's economy is in the hands
of three major players: the ANC, Business, and the workers
(labour).The discord in relationships between these players was
seen as likely to be constraining the country's economic growth
and prosperity.

Nevertheless, both business and government agreed that the
National Development Plan is the most significant research of its
kind so far produced in South Africa as it offers an accurate
diagnosis of the country's challenges and constraints. For this plan
to see the light of day, especially in the envisaged period of 17
years, these two parties would need to undertake to create a
genuine partnership and constructive dialogue. With the current
labour vigilance, especially in the mining sector, the urgency of
constructive dialogue cannot be doubted.

Youth Unemployment

Youth unemployment and the need for authentic development was
raised as an overarching issue, particularly because the country's
youth – who are leaders of tomorrow – are largely outside of
economic circles. The BLSA seems to have considered practical
steps to address at least some of the difficulties, which may be of

benefit, although these will remain ideas until they are thoroughly discussed and put into practice through effective dialogue and meeting of minds. This contention goes hand-in-hand with the issue of skill shortages, which appeared to be a source of pain for the business leaders I spoke with, who were often faced with employing school-leavers or even graduates who were not adequately prepared for the world of work or the open labour market. Requests were made for the reinvention of Further Education and Training Colleges.

The Mining Sector

As one of the strongest pillars of the South African economy, the mining sector has been plagued by labour and performance conflicts, as well as economic problems. Those I interviewed saw the bigger concern as the resistance to change in the culture of the mines. Furthermore, the black leaders who assume top leadership roles are put under pressure to, on one side, satisfy the mine owners' or shareholders expectations against the majority of the mine workers who also hold expectations of the black leaders in these top leadership roles. This pits the capitalist mentality of the mine owners to satisfy shareholders' expectations against workers' expectations of their new black leaders.

In addition, many mines are downsizing due to financial problems and industrial action. It appears that this has led to some fatal incidents, which have made media headlines. Furthermore, economically devastating mining strikes almost led to a country-wide recession. We have seen decisions by mines to downsize after strikes. The Marikana incident, as well as platinum mine strikes that lasted almost six months, have dented economic prospects for South Africa, and almost landed the economy into a recession. Authors such as Kahane (who has written extensively on the topic of management) posit that in such situations, honest and meaningful dialogue is the solution because the mentality of command and control does not work any longer. In the mining sector in particular where, to a large extent, the concept of command and control has been perpetuated, unions have seriously attacked this traditional approach and have, through dialogue between employers and employees, forced them to forge alternative leadership practices. The South African economy simply cannot afford a continuing downward spiral in its mining sector since mining supports a significant portion of the economy. Study participants agreed that the time had come for sincere and significant conversations to avoid prolonging this volatile situation, which can only be detrimental to the country's economy.

My participants' fears were that unless business and government were able to work effectively together, the NDP could become just another plan on paper, and that, to achieve success, mental and attitudinal shifts would be essential. In addition, the parties (both business and government) voiced their concern that these paradigm shifts need to be happening already. They simply cannot wait for another 17 years set out in the NDP if the country is to achieve its true potential. Prominent business scholars[25] commenting on similar issues from other parts of the global economy, where economic, social, and (to some extent) political circumstances called for a major shift in attitudes and mindset, posed these questions:

- What is the role of business leaders in society?
- What dominant logic is required to eradicate poverty at the bottom of the human pyramid?
- What kind of future does business want to be part of (vision)?
- The answers indicate a common theme – that finding solutions to these economic and social problems implies questioning traditional views as to why business exists and what its role is in eliminating poverty from the society within which it exists?

In 2008, Bill Gates addressed the World Economic Forum in Davos on the subject of creative capitalism, a methodology that both generates profits and seeks to redress the world's inequalities. In 2009, President Barack Obama said in his inauguration speech that the current state of the global economy was a consequence of greed and irresponsibility and a failure to make hard choices.[26]Around 2011, Klause Schwab (founder and executive chairman of the World Economic Forum)shared a view that in today's times, leadership is about being able to navigate within a larger, more complex set of issues that are also compounded by highly complicated relationships.[27]In 2018, South African president Cyril Ramaphosa, in his address at the United Nations General Assembly, said, "It is within our hands, as the leaders assembled here today, to forge a more representative, equal and fair United Nations that is empowered and equipped to lead the struggle to end poverty, unemployment and inequality in the world".[28]

While many of the world's societal, business, and political leaders are beginning to envision a new order and are listening to their consciences, the missing link seems to be what to change. Nonetheless, their concurrence that "quantum change in the way we live and work is urgently necessary"[29]is encouraging.

Returning to the South African situation, it would appear that our political and business leaders find themselves facing similar circumstances to those elsewhere in the world, where sustainability issues are also the focus of attention and may ultimately resolve the complex challenges facing humanity. This has in many ways become urgent for sustainable development which will ultimately resolve the complex challenges facing humanity today. There is a call for a "tripartite" relationship with government, business, and the community cooperatively working together.[30]The NDP may provide the driving force for this tripartite worldview, although it will be dependent on a genuine commitment to serious dialogue and taking into account the interests of all key stakeholders. Put differently, there is a need for a heightened level of consciousness for the sake of our country. This heightened level of consciousness will emphasize sustainable development, where economic and social progress as well as environmental protection are viewed as one. The guiding principle is that "unless leadership takes sustainability issues seriously, and embeds them in practice, leadership itself cannot be sustainable".[31] Unfortunately, in the case of South Africa, due to pressing issues related to both social and economic development, environmental protection is still elusive, even as the 21st century is stressing the need to earnestly consider the environment. Greed, corruption and unethical behaviour are a veritable plague within our country and will undoubtedly hamper progress in service delivery and the up-liftment of the economy. In recent times we have learned of the devastating erosion of the country's financial resources through what has come to be known as state capture. Although the NDP sets out to address corruption, only the rooting out of corruption, particularly at business and government levels, will enable us to tackle the problems holding up the resolution of humanitarian issues. Humanitarian issues include the ever-increasing divide between the rich and the poor, the powerful and the powerless. Sustainability can be genuinely realized when we are no longer grappling with overwhelms of poverty – when society can find its greatness in its courage to end poverty and protect its humanity, and the economy at large.

If leaders can demonstrate global stewardship, a superior model which could guide South Africa's tripartite structure to adopt higher moral ethics and responsibility will assist in the universal restoration and retention of lost societal trust. When launching the NDP, the Minister, Trevor Manuel, said:

> The plan we hand over today is about the actions that all of us must take to secure the future chartered in our Constitution. The plan is about our dreams and aspirations, and detailed actionable steps to achieve them…The Commission has been careful to distinguish between a broad strategy, specific policies of government and the day-to-day actions of business, government or

trade unions…The Commission realises that government on its own cannot improve living standards. It requires determined and measurable action by all social actors, and partnerships across society to raise living standards.[32]

Having considered the overall sentiments towards the plan and the acceptance of its strategies by business, government, and society, it would appear that South Africans, in general, are ready to rise to the challenge it offers.

Business leaders are beginning to realise there is indeed a need for a different approach and that the attitude that *the business of business is business* no longer applies. Socio-economic and environmental issues need to become legitimate concerns. Business seems ready and willing to take the action required for the rollout of the plan, as articulated in the BLSA blueprint. On the other hand, given the Presidency's comments, it seems there is a readiness to engage with all the relevant parties, including business. Nonetheless, what may stand in the way of successful implementation would be the distant and hostile, even artificial, historical relationship between business and government.

In my view, the biggest test will be who will take the initiative in terms of breaking through the past lack of trust. For any remarkable improvement to be realised, there has to be transparent, constructive and consistent dialogue that shows genuine stewardship and inclusivity. In my view, mere acknowledgement of the shortcomings, without taking the bold steps required to avoid perpetuating a destructive situation, would be futile. To echo President Obama's words, that failure or lack of courage to make hard choices could cost South Africa dearly in its attempt to shine as a beacon within the African continent. Some of the South Africans are already remarking on the failure of the ANC and government officials to make hard decisions and choices.

The NDP seeks to achieve both short-and long-term objectives rooted in the world of inclusive globalisation (WOIG) vision. This concept seeks to conduct profitable business through rooting out poverty and crime, lifting living standards, and providing health benefits, thereby addressing social ills.Crime and corruption remain some of the biggest threats to the South African economy and the possibility of eliminating negative factors linked with poverty.The findings of a study by Havenga, Mehana and Visagie in 2011(in which they studied the concept of leadership towards sustainable quality service delivery) revealed that a major South African problem is a lack of leadership capability, competence in governance and widespread corruption.[33]Although their findings certainly indicated that significant progress had been made in many areas, gains were still being reversed through a deficit of value-based leadership and the corruption that was and is still limiting the acceleration of a developmental local governance framework.

Chapter conclusion

The framework above provided a contextual basis for the discussion with the business leaders in my study. The outcome was a three-layered model that conceptualized the issues and challenges facing South African business as:

- being a new democracy
- becoming more of a global player and becoming even more prominent within the African continent
- meeting the challenges of the 21st century.
  The business leaders generally agreed that the NDP created an opportunity for the country to move forward in terms of:
- continuing to address the apartheid legacy
- creating more enlightened business practices, especially demonstrating a greater social and environmental conscience.

They also agree that for NDP outcomes to be achieved, business and government needed to forge more trusting relationships so as to work together in partnership.

Finally, they expressed concern regarding the dark cloud of corruption and state capture that has the potential, if not dealt with effectively, to endlessly slow the country's progress.

3

THE EMERGING MENTAL MODELS

GIVEN THAT MY RESEARCH was qualitative, comprising intense interviews with business leaders or captains of industry, this chapter will share some direct quotes in which they express their observations on their lived experiences of business in this global era. The aim was to seek to understand the meaning of their personal constructs as business leaders in South Africa. Their emergent mental models were studied by looking into their shared stories and identifying coherent meanings or key messages that were apparent. The process of consolidating these messages into themes involved critical analysis and interpretation of their individual narratives.

The participating business leaders were chief executives from various industries: including mining, telecommunication, investments, banking, and transport. There was also one representative from the Presidency. Their input was thematically analysed and coded to reveal the mental models. These mental models were used as fundamental pillars in forming a comprehensive business framework or model that could be adopted by 21st-century businesses to guide their journeys to true sustainability.

Both theoretical and practical aspects were considered.

Below are some of the sentiments that were expressed by the business leaders:

Business Leader 1: "I think to start off we have to trace back to where we come from, you know, from a pre-democracy time in our country where we were a closed economy and we were shielded from global competition and we didn't have to worry about foreign investors…So the dawn of democracy and the new issues we are grappling with, we had to accept the new paradigms. Those paradigms meant that big companies like Old Mutual, SA Breweries, AECI, Tiger Brands, etc. had to look outward all of a sudden. That brought a challenge to the whole industry- a lot of challenges for the captains of industry where they suddenly had to think globally instead of locally. To give an example, that is the time when companies like SA Breweries, Di Data, Anglo American, Old Mutual started going for offshore listings to raise capital in foreign markets in order to invest offshore and buy companies overseas. Some got it right, but others burnt their fingers very badly."

Business Leader 3: "SA business cannot compete globally if we remain small…For us to play in emerging market space, SA has created a microcosm of virtually anything in the world."

Business Leader 4: "For the past 10 years or so our growth has been driven by consumer spending without a lot of investment on infrastructure. Unfortunately, some of these actions have put pressure on infrastructure e.g. roads, electricity, malls cropping up, putting pressure on municipalities and now we are trying to play catch-up."

Business Leader 2: "What is required for SA companies to be global players is essentially an understanding of how the global stage works. In other words, we have to adopt some of the principles and practices of being a global player. It doesn't mean that we don't have our own challenges. If we look, for instance, the fact that as a country we have the high level of youth unemployment, and that we have probably the highest Gini coefficients in the world where the gap between the haves and the have-nots or the have-lots is still as high as it is in this country, means that we also face exactly some of the same ills that some of the global companies face."

Business Leader 3: "As South African business, we have taken advantage of the fact that our economy has become open and has created opportunities for ourselves as a country. So if one looks at SA business today. I mean, clearly we have enjoyed the benefits of this democracy immensely … So there are certainly a large number of pockets where South African companies within certain sectors have done really well over the last 18 years, even though there may be sectors where we have lagged behind."

Business Leader 5: "Affiliation by SA to the World Economic Forum where SA is playing a key role; SA being invited to be a member of the G20 and B20 which is the business component that runs along G20, this has created perceptions that we are a country that can add in some of these debates and discussion."

Business Leader 6: "Now, I think we still have a challenge, because I don't think we have consciously indoctrinated our workers to realise that this is our country. Yes, there is a reality that has never changed. The owners of the factors of production are still white people . . . . But how do you then talk to the parastatals that are a hundred percent owned by the state, that failed to succeed, that have black bureaucrats that are leading them? How do you talk to that? They fail because of the absence of that political consciousness. They fail because of the absence of that redirection of the worker force in those parastatals to have a consciousness that seek to say, 'This belongs to us'."

Government Leader 7: We all need to have a different mind shift, whether you are a unionist, or government leader, or business leader. It seems that the attitudes are just not aligned and therefore we are not pulling in the same direction and that poses a lot of risk."

Below are some extracts from the business leaders:

Business Leader 1: The volatile global business scene is increasingly characterized by turbulence, unpredictability, chaos, and complexity. Our challenges are many since becoming a democracy. Complexities are huge, not only for government but for us business leaders. We need to think outside the box. For us to be sustainable as businesses, we need to always be able to reinvent our models – business models. What worked 20 years ago does not necessarily work today. The very business that I'm running herein South Africa is facing tremendous challenges from a competition perspective. A lot of our competitors don't have bricks and mortar here. You know, they fly in and fly – they work out of suitcases so their cost bases are very low. They are not committed to this country; they can pack and go any time.

Business Leader 2: Due to the realities of the industry we are operating in (asset management), one always has to look at the global environment because we are a global player. As South Africa, we get affected by all these volatilities in investments, volatilities in currencies.

Business Leader 3: Since the 1994 transformation into democracy, South Africa has become a player in the African continent. Becoming a democracy and key role player in African context comes with complexities and responsibilities; South Africa is co-responsible for some of the UN's peacekeeping activities on the continent because it is in the country's best interest that the continent remains stable.

Business Leader 4: Key uncertainties impacting South Africa on all levels of sustainability:
- There are many people crossing the borders into South Africa, people that are going to need medical care, pensions, housing, etc.
- Escalating social bills in terms of grants for children, grants for disabled people, etc.

- Escalating grants for unemployed people.
- Our social bill in terms of grants has gone through the roof. Every year they allocate more, and more, but we are battling to keep up. It's a burden on the individuals that are working – so our challenges are many since becoming a democracy. Complexities are huge, not only for government but for us as business leaders ... we need always be able to reinvent our business models.
- In the 21st century, service must be customer-driven and customised according to what the client wants. Our economy is still not led by customer demands for products or services; we still do not deliver within the shortest possible time and we are not driven by population growth and needs. This limits our economic growth and our attainment of world-class performance.
- The future cannot be sustainable if businesses don't constantly re-invent and re-evaluate themselves.

Significant Emergent Themes

Figure 8 is a diagram that presents a succinct view of the themes that emerged. These themes were identified as significant for a business to be successful in the 21st century. They are in no particular order.

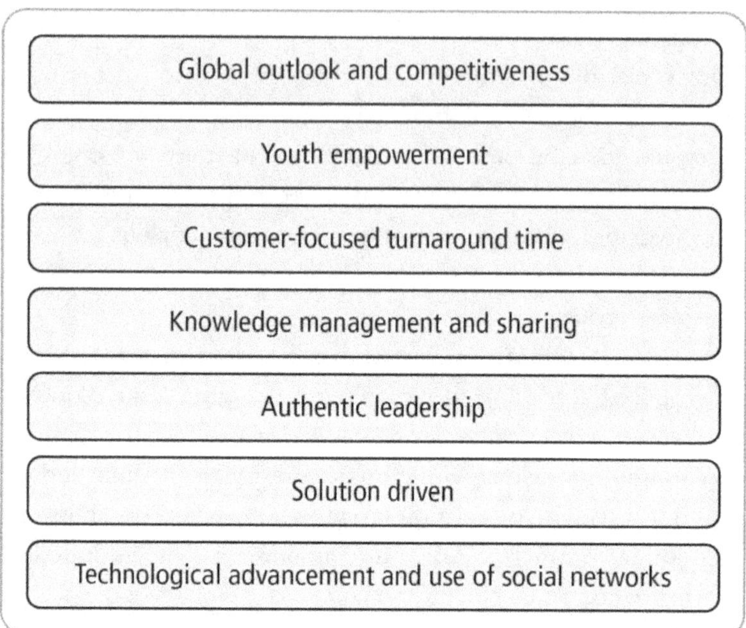

Figure 8: Significant themes

Global Outlook and Competitiveness

Globalisation is clearly an overarching reality for many businesses and was a key aspect for the industry leaders I spoke with. Relationships are being forged through global interconnections at an unprecedented rate and are reshaping the context for many business activities. This was expressed by the first business leader (as noted above), when he said, "We have to trace back to where we come from, the pre-democracy time: a period in our country when we were a closed economy, where we didn't have to worry about foreign investors…where we were shielded from global competition, and we could also not invest in other global markets, we were forced to look inwards."

A similar statement was echoed by **Business Leader 4**, "South Africa is now tied to the rest of the world, mainly Europe and the

US and is now starting to shift to China. 'When those markets cough, we catch the cold' as the saying goes". The result of this new process of interconnectivity and relationships results in unclear boundaries within and between organisations, nations, and global interests.[34]The implications of this are best expressed by BLSA, which defines "competitive" as being able and ready to project local business on a global scale.

Another very significant aspect of business, heightened through globalisation and the interconnectedness that has come along with it, is the rising level of complexity in business. **Business leader 3**, supports this view when he says:

> I sit on two global boards, the Anglo PLC and BP PLC and I'm always amazed how, Michael Friedman, who's one of BP's partners in Russia, will just make a statement somewhere else in the north part of Russia, and in five minutes, you know it's something material, everybody knows it…it immediately impacts the share price…so the organisation always has to be geared to be able to react and be malleable far more rapidly than was the case 10 years ago…things move at lightning speed and if you are a listed company that makes a big issue.

The world has indeed become smaller and more interconnected. All the industry leaders appreciated that globalisation would immediately pose challenges to South Africa in terms of speed, the capacity to learn and engage with the rest of the world, as well as their readiness to operate on a global scale. Below is what some of these industry leaders had to say about their experiences:

Business Leader 5: "What is required for companies to be global players is essentially an understanding of how the global stage works…it's absolutely important to have the employees that understand what it means to be a global player, that you have to play not by your own rules but by the rules of the world as it were."

Business Leader 4: "I think for business and leaders, the test is going to be on their ability to see opportunities, and how quickly they act on those opportunities, because I don't think they are going to present themselves in the same way they did historically, and their ability to embrace change …."

Business Leader 3: "To compete in the 21st century you really have to be highly nimble and tuned in, because everything that happens impacts you now … the worldview has become an important part of your vision and your position in the 21st century."

Business Leader 1: "Complexities are many since we became a global player as South Africa. Complexities are huge not only for government but for business as well. We need to think outside the box, for us to be sustainable as business, we need to always be able to reinvent our models – business models."

The implications of globalisation are clearly reshaping the playing fields for business, including improved economies of scale for effective competition. As an example, Business Leader 1 shared his experiences that his company achieved economies of scale through expanding outside South Africa. Today, this particular company is 30–40% bigger, mainly because it gained additional value from outside the country.SAB Miller established itself internationally and today it is seen as a British company listed on the London Stock Exchange. Since listing, SAB has continued to expand and has steadily consolidated its position as a global brewing company. With strategic acquisitions around the world, it has focused on operating improvements and efficiencies for at least the last decade. The SAB case reveals a company that managed to transfer skills and competencies into other developing countries in a way that their counterparts from the developed world could not. They built on the strong performance management culture they had developed at home, which became a critical strength in their successful turning around of previously state-owned failing breweries in Africa, China and Central Europe.[35]

The industry leaders I spoke with mentioned that skills have become easily available across continents. Business Leader 1 noted that organisations are able to source talent from anywhere in the world since companies have become multinational. This message was also articulated in an article in *Business Week* authored by Beverley Fearis in 2005 where she indicates that in present times, a leader might be from India, working for an Indian-owned company, but be assigned to work in the United States. Another may be from France, working for an Australian-owned company and living in China.[36]With the world as we know it now, it is clear that globalisation has indeed resulted in the absence of national borders and barriers to trade among nations. Globalisation has grown to be associated with the shift in traditional patterns of international production, investment, and flow of capital, goods, information, and people among dissimilar nations.[37]

As in most countries these days, jobs will no longer be for life, and employees, even top executives, are now considered assets to be used as and when needed, and discarded when not. Acquiring critical skills across borders on defined contractual terms has become commonplace in South Africa. **Business Leader 3** echoed this when he said:

> Staying ahead of the curve and getting the best possible brains is absolutely pivotal…you have to get the best skill in the world…all multinationals have become multinational in constituency inside the companies as well. I mean Citibank is being run by a guy from India, Pepsi is being run by a woman from India, I am on the BP Board, and the chairman is Swedish, etc.

He further stressed that local companies need to realise that unless they act similarly, South African companies will not be able to successfully compete in the 21st century.

An additional aspect, raised by industry leaders 1 and 5, related to the way of conducting business in the global economy. **Business Leader 1** shared some personal experiences, being a black leader within the mining industry:

> I have to think about my success as a leader. I have to think about having a job, retaining my job. I have to think about satisfying the expectations of my employers. I have another element to that, the people that I am working amongst who have high expectations of me – because the majority are black labourers …Now I have to look at the influential layer, which is mainly white. Now I have to look at that and say to myself – I have to work with these people, they must support me…so what must I do? I must actually be a kind of leader that can penetrate, and then get to these people and drive the message….[The] Minister of Labour enforces that companies give business to black people…I have the chairman and the board for whom I am running the business…I have to go back to the shareholders who want profits…

This business leader was expressing his frustration at having to deal with different stakeholders who often had conflicting expectations of him, including white people who believed they had a better way of running the mines. Mines have been particularly slow to embrace the changes that accompanied the new democracy and elements remain who are unwilling to alter their beliefs .In the mining industry, the majority of employees at lower levels are black and they have high expectations of the black managers who now lead the mines, creating challenges not only in terms of effective communication but also their desire to build a new mining culture. These black leaders are charged with the need to somehow ensure that mines survive as productive businesses, even as the environments within seem to be misaligned with the changes occurring in broader South African and global contexts.

Business Leader 3 also highlighted the importance of culture, although from a different perspective. In his narrative, he explained that he saw culture as a significant business element, capable of being manipulated to inculcate either certain means of doing things or particular ways of thinking about business, even in multinational companies. He used the example of a South African company keeping its cultural roots, even when employing executive managers with different perspectives, ensuring that the "home" culture permeated throughout, so as to retain its original DNA. Culture, as a phenomenon is known to fundamentally inform or influence the way people live or behave, and in turn within a business, it influences the environment through its employees. The concept of culture and multiculturism is therefore of special significance in the current era because, through globalisation, South Africa is being ever more exposed to cultural differences.

Another strong need related to globalisation expressed by business leaders is for a heightening of awareness regarding the global context and a deepening of international relations as South African businesses begin considering worldwide investment.

South Africa is also "starting to play a key role in the international forum – being invited to be a member of the G20 and B20, which is the business component that runs alongside the G20" (Business Leader 5). Through these developments, we are adding value in the international arena.

What is Required from South African businesses?

What is required from South African businesses is, firstly, to learn from emerging economies. As a developing country, South Africa can certainly learn from other emerging economies such as Brazil, Russia, India, and China. These countries seem to have claimed legitimate global recognition within a relatively short time span.

Secondly, it would be of significant value if South Africa sharpened its attempts in understanding the big picture as it navigates its way into the global business spaces.

Thirdly, business leaders here need to get to grips with the rationale and realities of the global marketplace, as well as the role of BRICS countries, of which South Africa is now a member, given the prominent role being played with regard to the continent. As they create their business visions, they need to take into account the significance, not only of the African context, but also of the world as a whole, including the interconnectedness of the various economies of the world.[38]Together, global interconnections and the relationships they forge represent a historically unprecedented process that is rapidly reshaping the contexts for many activities. This results in boundaries within and between nations and global interests becoming more and more unclear or undefined.

At broader national level, we know that even big business is facing internal and external issues, including limiting policies at government level, the implication being that business leaders are being thrust into survival mode. They must be increasingly versatile as they juggle a plethora of demands and risks. Since not all businesses will have a multinational vision, various other opportunities will need to be explored.

Nevertheless, global business acumen encompasses the ability to comprehend the business environment in its totality. Cohen, who is a renowned author on leadership effectiveness, has provided critical competency areas for global leaders:[39]

- Successful global leaders need to develop global business knowledge that includes being technologically perceptive, demonstrating financial acumen, and being skilled in the areas of strategic marketing, enterprise knowledge, organisational behaviour, and operations management.
- Successful global leaders should demonstrate basic values such as integrity, excellence, respect, and perseverance. In addition, they should have a thirst for learning, acceptance of difference,

a desire to understand others and the ability to remain authentic. Authenticity was consistently referred to in discussions with my study participants.

Fourthly, while the international economy still features massive global companies, large numbers of newcomers are small and medium enterprises (SMEs) who are internationally active.[40]SMEs are key players in the economy and the wider organisational ecosystem. Enabling them to adapt and thrive in a more open environment and participate more actively in both the economic space and transformational agendas will boost economic growth and deliver a more inclusive globalisation. SMEs have an important role to play in achieving the Sustainable Development Goals (SDGs), by promoting inclusive and sustainable economic growth, providing employment and decent work for all, promoting sustainable industrialisation and fostering innovation, and reducing income inequalities.

The role of SMEs at local, regional, national and even international levels has not been extensively studied, nor is it well understood, since their strategies do not all conform to current theories or conceptual frameworks. The SME policy space is complex.[41]Since SMEs are often embedded in local ecosystems, which represent their primary source of knowledge, skills, finance, business opportunities and networks, it is important to consider local factors and how national policies are tailored to these conditions, as well as how they coordinate with regional and territorial policies.[42]

Customer-focused Fast Turnaround Time

Turnaround time was a highly prized factor mentioned by all the business leaders I spoke to, along with customer focus. **Business Leader 1** said, "We need to change the way we do things. Today's clients want solutions. They don't want products, they want solutions to their problems – to their business problems… Today's customer service model is very different from that of years past. People do not want the same things they used to. Thus, it is logical that today's business does not either."

This same message was strongly echoed by business leaders 4 and 5, in that, because they are more informed and have a wider choice, they want to do business where customers can be attracted, delighted and retained. Participant 4 alluded to Chinese industry: "Chinese are known throughout the world for customer-focused service. If you want a R100 phone, they will do a R100 phone for you. If you want a R10,000 phone, they will give you a R10,000 phone, and anything in between."

Business leaders 1, 3, and 4 emphasized that winning organisations are those that are proactive and ready to adopt new business models while creating a superior service perception in their customers.

Customers want speed, efficiency, technology, instant gratification and to continually raise the bar. **Business Leader 1** said:

Technology has become a business tool that could be harnessed to the advantage of the business. In other words, all of a sudden we were all carrying mobile devices (cell phones).I mean you can conduct your meetings around the clock, conduct business conversations while you are travelling in a car or in another city. So technology became very much a part of us…at a corporate level, staff have to be up-skilled with the new technologies, a better way of doing business at a cheaper cost.

The same business leader also noted, "Technology allows us to do video conference facilities…I don't have to go to London all the time."

As explained by all the industry leaders, it is *being able to change direction quickly at the onset of new information* that enables business survival. For instance, a business leader could be absorbing essential new information in Asia today, in America tomorrow and be back in Africa at the weekend. The industry leaders concurred that leaders had to be "tuned in" and quick to react because the world has become smaller.

Anticipation of changes, and therefore appropriate action, was seen as pivotal. Business Leader 3 called this being nimble.

Solution-driven

Closely linked with the concept of customer-focused turnaround time is the importance of being solution-driven. The industry leaders were emphatic that clients need solutions. They stressed that business needs to reinvent itself to accurately predict and understand customer requirements and customise offerings tailored to bold solutions. The different motor industries compete on value creation, as well as through extending motor service plans and offering vehicle features that compete with more expensive brands. Many industry experts have suggested that perhaps it is time for better business strategies,[43] with one of them (Jackson) even suggesting a new knowledge-based framework called Customer Value Exchange (CVE). This would enable companies to increase market share and grow profitability by applying more effective information management and marketing techniques. CVE encompasses a suite of information and decision technologies that analyse business operations, customers, and market potential in order to optimally allocate resources to create value for customers. Jackson notes that the transportation industry (e.g. airlines, cruise ships, and rail carriers) has implemented a quantitative process called yield management and that telecommunications has a network optimisation procedure. Banks are also beginning to differentiate their product and service offerings by leveraging technology, such as banking applications, ATMs, call centres and internet-based PC applications.

All clients require solutions at some level, and this has become a business reality. Even for non-profit organisations, there is always some stakeholder requirement that seeks satisfaction.

Empowering the Youth

Issues of empowerment were raised from various perspective by the leaders in my study. However, from their personal experiences of employing young people, potential future leaders, they specifically raised the importance of empowering the youth. Since they recognised that tomorrow's leaders will inevitably be charged with leading on a very different playing field, they felt there must be an increasing awareness of how the new generation thinks and what drives them. First Rand was used as an example of this, having deliberately adopted an empowering culture where talented youngsters are supported in expressing themselves, in introducing new technologies and in driving innovation, particularly in the internet banking arena. Cohen asserted that there are two types of leaders: those who use the best talent, and those who develop it: "The successful global leaders understand that developing talent is top priority."[44] Therefore, executives need to contribute to the leadership pipeline through intentional influence: "Mentoring, coaching and teaching are three primary roles that leaders must master."[45]

Similarly, Business Leader 6 referred to a mining initiative where youngsters who understand the market or the marketability of platinum are posted abroad, for example to Singapore, Tokyo, Shanghai, or Delhi. Their project will be to study the platinum market and to return with advice on the latest trends and expertise in plants and smelters. This will enable local production without dependence on costly international skills. In addition, this impacts the South African economy, avoiding the necessity for reciprocal importation of high volumes of low-valued goods, rather offering opportunities for negotiating more favourable rates. **Business**

Leader 4 shared his perspective: "Leaders around the world are getting younger and younger ... In corporates, if you look at a lot of the European companies, a lot of people who are senior are in their 40s ....Generally a lot of things are starting to change where there's dynamism, and maybe shareholders are realising that an old man who may be too set in his... own ways is not going to help."

Loughlin and Barling concurred when they wrote that it would be a big mistake if organisations were to continue ignoring young workers, for two main reasons. Firstly, young people represent a large portion of the population, including as part-time workers, and part-time work has become increasingly common. Secondly, young people are strongly influenced by their work environments, principally because attitudes and aspirations are established as teenagers or young adults. According to Loughlin and Barling, industrial-organisational research has revealed that:

Younger workers derive most satisfaction from opportunities to use their current skills and to develop new skills. Without having a chance to shine at work, they become cynical and disinterested.

Young workers are a valuable resource. Their educational levels tend to be higher than those of their parents and they are more sophisticated technologically, therefore viewing the world from a global rather than a domestic perspective. In addition, multicultural environments have engendered an open-mindedness that was rare in earlier generations.[46]

Despite this, much entry-level paid work consists of menial activities, leading to disillusionment and demotivation. More recent research on the so-called millennials indicates that even though they may lack hard-core business skills when entering the labour market, they have a multitude of skills to be applied. Interestingly, millennials expressed excitement about possibilities to acquire meaning and to feel valued through projects they found important and which offered them recognition. They wanted what they called a "positive buzz" in their jobs.[47]Their desire is to contribute. The young millennial generation expects a workplace where their leaders will not merely promote the organisation's vision, they need them to demonstrate interest in the personal aspirations and visions of young people. Youngsters want to be innovators – they are mastering continually evolving technology and gadgets. Constant change does not threaten them; indeed, they find it exhilarating. They enjoy the journey to becoming smarter, faster, and better, whether at work or outside. Many of them act as technical "consultants" to family and friends.[48]

People no longer want to work for leaders who are authoritarian and micro-managers. They crave empowerment, someone with vision who can lift them "to higher sights, raise a person's performance to a higher standard, building a personality beyond its normal limitations."[49]

Against this background, more recent research in 2017 suggested that millennials in South African still perceived the country as politically and socially fragmented and were pessimistic about the prospects for progress, along with concerns about safety, social inequality and environmental sustainability. They felt that business was not sufficiently prioritizing issues that mattered to them, particularly with regard to education and skills acquisition.

Therefore organisations would be well advised to develop a genuine understanding of each generation as well as the challenges the different generations bring to the workplace in terms of communication style, career aspirations, and knowledge transfer.[50]

Knowledge Management and Information Sharing

Knowledge management has become one of the dominant features of the 21st century. Therefore, the ability to gain access to and harness information has become crucial for many organisations. Nevertheless, data acquisition and management remains a challenge for business in general, including dealing with information complexity.[51]

The industry leaders I interviewed all stressed the overwhelming nature of information and they felt South Africans were not yet completely au fait with information management. One specifically mentioned the lack of focus on both skills and knowledge generation and management in agriculture, fisheries, mining and forestry.

It was admitted by the leaders that for the business sector (as a global player) there are implications of virtual, real-time information flows, and South Africa will have to adopt these as well.

Business Leader5 said a major danger for both business and government was the lack of critical skills research and knowledge that could take the country forward: "If we don't have the kind of skills that are going to make us competitive in the 21st century, we'll be going backwards as a country and as companies within the country, and that is the biggest risk we face."

Authentic Leadership

Genuine authenticity in leadership was another theme that assumed high significance with my participating business leaders. They stressed the need for leaders to address social questions as they relate to business issues, in addition to their focus on profit and sustainability. Five individuals, in particular, acknowledged that business appears to be hardly concerned with social up-liftment or the longer-term survival of society. **Business Leader 1** said: "It is important to become a leader with a conscience and not just look at profits, but also look at sustaining and ploughing back into the society."

Business Leader 5 echoed this: "We often have talked about people-centricity, but very often we don't do much about that."

Business Leader 6 further highlighted a necessity for what he calls "the quasi-governmental entities" to have a more progressive philosophy, less about lining their own pockets and more about developing critical skills to turn South Africa around.

Mention was again made of the lack of trust between business and government: "The lack of trust between business and government is a huge issue. Given our history and our past, the baggage that we all carry, government and business especially, need to do a lot more work to build this trust, to understand that our fortunes are tied at the hip."

Business Leader 3 expanded on this:

This non-talking between government and companies, it also affects the expansion outside because when Sarkozy jumps on a plane and goes to China, he takes with him the top 20 industrialists from France. By the time he lands in China they know what they want. Airbus is there, the nuclear guys are there, etc. It's a government initiative, but there's no bone about it, everybody understands that France is looking for business in China. We don't have that here, because it's dysfunctional. When the President of RSA goes to China (for an example), he should be going with top 20 industrialists from South Africa, but because of this distrust and the politics, it doesn't happen. The President ends up going with 200 shopkeepers from NAFCOC, and you've seen those trips, there's so many of them and it doesn't work.

Business Leader 7 asserted that all the players needed a significant mind shift: "Whether you are a unionist, or a government leader, or a business leader, it seems to me that the attitudes are not aligned and therefore we are not pulling in the same direction and this is pulling us back."

Overall, it was seen as essential to cultivate and maintain authenticity in dialogue and action to enable business and government to deal with the distrust that clouded the ability to confront and overcome the challenges facing the country as a whole. The leaders also raised a red flag regarding labour unrest, in the form of strike action taking a toll on the South African economy.

Technological Advancement and the Use of Social Networks

All the leaders in my study agreed that, over the last decade, technology has extensively permeated business, governmental, and other sectors throughout the world and has become indispensable to effective operation. **Business Leader 5** said:

> It has become imperative for us as companies in a global environment, to keep up with the developments in technology, and adopt those and use them, because technological tools have become increasingly important tools that companies must use to communicate with their stakeholders, not just shareholders – so we communicate with our employees, customers, creditors, suppliers and with society as a whole.

For business in South Africa, the dilemma seems to be the ability to keep pace with technological usage and advancement, including for communication with stakeholders, both locally and abroad. For example, transportation is the backbone of the South African economy and the use of social networks, such as Twitter and Facebook, has become an integral part of Prasa's means of staying in communication with its passengers. Similarly, FNB (First National Bank) was well recognised for its exceptional communication through its smartphone applications.

Interactions with organisations are posted on the internet, primarily through social networks such as Facebook and Twitter, and those which are unaware of what is being reported could have their reputations sullied overnight. During the presentation of the NDP, minister Trevor Manuel highlighted that science and technology have shaped, and will continue to shape, opportunities for humanity in general, including the poorer nations.

It is generally recognised that innovation is essential for a middle-income country, such as South Africa, to progress to high-income status. Remarkable changes have overtaken workplaces worldwide, particularly in the technological sense, and predominantly with regards to information and communications. In this area, globalism has become both a cause and a consequence of sustained change.[52]

Mainly as a direct result of rapid technical advancement, the socio-technological fabric of home and work settings has been revolutionised. This has, at least in part, created expectations and has helped fuel the greed leading to crime and corruption. As early as 2011, writers such as Nel and Beudeker warned of the consequences of businesses and organisations not keeping up with technology: "If the business is still wondering what to do about the essentials of 24/7, wireless, and real-time interconnectivity, they will be out of competition rapidly."[53]

In my reading, one writer (Nordstrom)claims that by 2020 we will no longer be talking of the information age from a technological point of view, but we will be entering the *"age of imagination"*.[54] It is no longer uncommon to have our lives regulated via cellphone-linked watches, tablets and gadgets that are linked to our lifestyles and daily activities. The idea of face calling, as an example, has become a norm for people as a way of staying in contact. In today's world, we have computer devices that can be worn around our arms that read our blood pressure and other health factors in real time.

Some foresee that in the near future we might have personalised computing devices implanted in our arms that track our movements, reminding us of appointments and keeping track of our health status. As you get into your car, your personal device automatically switches over to the standard on-board communication system. At my home, for example, the security system is attached through my own tablet, which allows me to view the inside and outside yard of my house from my office.

I think what we see today is already giving an indication that the probability of a technology-driven lifestyle is shifting to a higher gear. With the 4thIndustrial Revolution and the fast-paced technology age that is emerging, the convergence of microbiology with computer-chip technology in our daily lives could be common cause in another decade or so. Think about this probability!

In South Africa, technological advancement has challenged business mainly from a financial perspective, forcing it to keep up with the latest technologies and the ever-increasing pace of change throughout the world. This has been exacerbated by the emergence of social networks and gadgets that enable worldwide communication conveniently and around the clock. The general message regarding technology and social networks is that the best strategy lies in adopting and using whatever is available, because they have become increasingly important tools for companies to conduct business. The reality of the ever-speeding technological advancement across the world was echoed in the 2019 World Economic Forum meeting in Davos. On the agenda was how countries could respond to and shape changes in how goods were produced, distributed and consumed. The question arises from the fact that the world is entering a fourth industrial revolution, where a new wave of technological progress will launch us into a new era of globalisation.

Chapter Conclusion

It is a given that in the new era that is calling for sustainable management, business is or will soon be forced to shift gear into thinking about issues of sustainability, or rather how to merge sustainable management with issues of profitability and globalism to remain competitive.

Our economy will be shaken from different perspectives (socially, economically, politically, and technologically).Business in South Africa is having to grapple with these global challenges while local challenges are still a prominent feature in business. There is vast literature on the topics of leadership in the 21st century and the concept of globalisation. However, very little focuses on highlighting how these immediate global circumstances are shaping business leaders' mental models and perspectives of the future. The voice of business has been and still remains low key.

4

MAKING SENSE OF THE IDENTIFIED THEMES AND MENTAL MODELS

AS AN EXTENSION of the previous chapter wherein mental models and current challenges were dealt with, the focus of this chapter moves towards the actions required to deal with those challenges lying ahead, as described in the visions and mental models of those leaders in my study. What was notable during the discussions with the business leaders was that even though we are already in the 21st century, it is still within the early stages of the century, thus some of the challenges coming along with it have begun emerging globally. However, it is envisaged that more challenges will probably still emerge as the 21st century matures.

Future Perspectives of Sustainability in the South African Context

An in-depth review of sustainability from business and environmental perspectives.

Sustainability strategies are clearly emerging to support traditional business goals. There is growing pressure for organisations to take environmental sustainability issues more seriously, and some have actually integrated these concerns with

59

more familiar business imperatives. While environmental questions are beginning to take a place alongside the need for profit maximization, cost reduction, growing revenue, and improvements in quality, in order to embrace practices that legitimize sustainable management, business appears to still be somewhat uncertain as to how to effectively achieve these objectives. The intent may be voiced, but specific initiatives are sometimes not concretized and require more specificity and commitment to guarantee inclusion in futuristic endeavours.

Having said this, in South Africa, it would appear that social and environmental sustainability measures have mainly fallen into the category of corporate social responsibility'.[55]My personal view is that if sustainability is regarded as a critical necessity, it should instead be legitimized by taking a valid place alongside time-honoured standard strategic plans. At this stage, the intent can be heard from the way business leader's talk, but their current strategic initiatives seem to still need further plantation and inclusion in the futuristic endeavours.

KPMG revealed in 2008 that implementing, managing and reporting on social responsibility efforts had become almost an expected organisational phenomenon, in that 73% of the largest global companies worldwide had adopted responsibility goals. However, KMPG also disclosed that some organisations had undertaken initiatives merely as a defensive response to external forces such as stakeholders, or even regulation pressures in an effort to retain legitimacy and image. Where this is the case, the lack of genuine buy-in will undermine the progress towards long-term sustainability.[56]It is important to emphasise, however, that if this is indeed the general premise on which business regards the corporate social responsibly initiative without genuine buy into it, it will undermine progress and long-term sustainability will thus suffer.

On the other hand, Baskin (who has prominently written on aspects of corporate social responsibility) discovered that while it is undeniable that corporate responsibility efforts are somewhat superficial, these initiatives are not necessarily lower in developing countries and that there has been a remarkable rise in corporate responsibility even in emerging markets.[57]Moreover, corporate responsibly is more likely to be found in economies with globally active companies (multinationals), with democratic political structures and with NPOs (Non Profit Organisations) or NGOs (Non Governmental Organisations. Baskin reported that not only are developing countries taking an active interest in corporate responsibility/sustainability issues, a number (especially in South African and Brazil) are among the global leaders in this trend.

This implies that there is fertile ground for intensifying these efforts and benefits to be gained for SA business, its economy and society in general. It is my belief that, to reach maximum sustainability, organisations in this country must examine the value they add, as a trade-off between taking care of financial health and also the social/environmental/ethical health of the business in relation to the broader societal and economic health of the country.

Business leaders can view sustainability-driven imperatives from three different perspectives: pragmatic, moral, and cognitive. *Pragmatic* refers to the extent to which they believe these contribute to reduced costs, such as through improved resource efficiency, to reduced risk of legal liability, to enhanced reputation or image or to any other factors that make a realistic business case. *Moral legitimacy* refers to "the right thing to do", regardless of costs or other benefits to the business. *Cognitive sustainability* refers to what makes sense to individuals, for example, what will make their jobs easier in the long run. Sustainability endeavours may potentially disrupt traditional business procedures and thus increase the complexity of managerial decision-making. However, they may also help streamline decision-making in the long run, standardise stakeholder interactions, clarify cultural values and resolve any cognitive dissonance among conscientious managers or even reduce burdens imposed by regulation.[58]Leadership should explore and manage these potential scenarios to create positive attitudes throughout the organization. Based on existing literature, it is evident that attitudes towards various elements of sustainability affect legitimacy and, in turn, legitimacy affects the behaviours within organisations and may either hamper or facilitate the success of sustainability undertakings. Such insights or even attitudes could help facilitate the transformation of profit-seeking commercial enterprises into effective vehicles for promoting the protection, restoration, and growth of natural and social capital which is a necessary condition for achieving a truly sustainable economy.[59]Sustainability is part and parcel of globalization and the 21st century and it can no longer be overlooked or shied away from.

Sustainable economies will, in the long run, facilitate sustainable businesses. These two concepts are inextricably entwined.

Figure 9 depicts an ideal relationship for these concepts of social responsibility, sustainability and the NDP, given the South African situation.

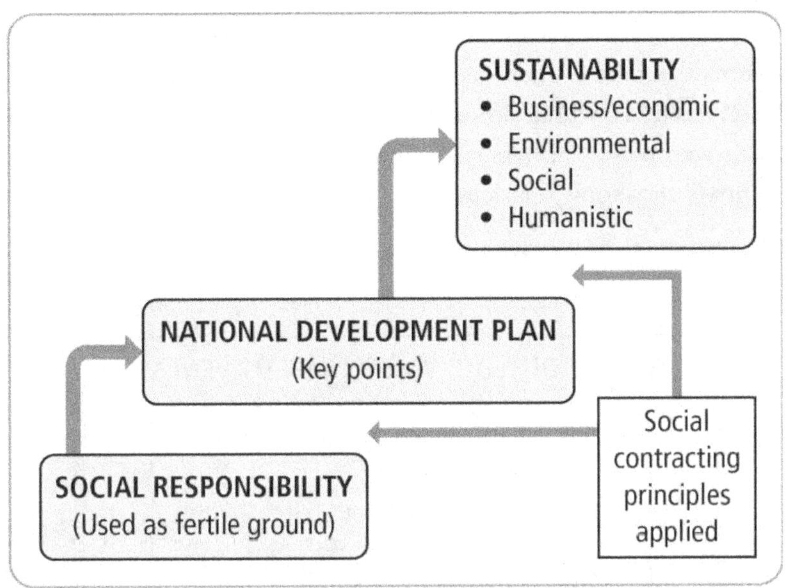

Figure 9: The relationship between social responsibility, the National Development Plan and sustainability

South Africa's unique circumstances and the reality of it being a new player in worldwide issues means environmental sustainability needs further engagement between key stakeholders, in spite of its position as a leader in pursuing corporate social responsibility. Sustainability should no longer be confined to social responsibility platforms, but must deliberately become a significant topic on boardroom agendas. To thrive, and even survive, legitimising holistic sustainability has become a business imperative and requires a multi-pronged approach. Indeed, the South African government has become involved in environmental issues, such as global warming.

However, perhaps a valid starting point for pursuing business sustainability lies in the already existing grounds of corporate social responsibility. For this country, the National Development Plan, being based on economic, social, and environmental concerns, may become the vehicle to drive engagement between business, government and civil society. The thinking that could facilitate legitimate initiative/undertakings towards achieving sustainability in the 21st century within a South African context (wherein business and government form part of the critical pillars of moving the country's economy) is encapsulated in the framework/model below.

Figure 10: Sustainability achievement model

Depending on the nature of that business, its strategic intent, and reasons for existence, this framework could facilitate both effective thinking and dialogue around concepts, dilemmas, and potential risks that require decisiveness and efficient decision making by leadership. In my view, this framework could serve as a guideline for a sustainable business of the 21st century.

To be maximally fruitful, principles of sound governance would be crucial, particularly in respect of those themes brought to the fore by the industry leaders in my survey, including authenticity.

The implementation of the National Development Plan will succeed only if both government and business work as an integrated team to authentically reshape the economy. This is but one example, and closer scrutiny of the themes raised by the leaders illustrates that the glue for the process indisputably lies in the application of sound governance principles by all parties.

Sound governance has increasingly come under the spotlight here as mismanagement has been unveiled in both corporate and government spheres, in spite of the King reports, which have provided best-practice principles for directors, executives, and regulators alike. The third King report received both local and international recognition for its contributions and guidelines towards corporate governance. With the country's economy at stake, abiding by these provisions would be crucial. This second model (figure 10) suggests a comprehensive approach, relevant in the 21st century that could be adopted by leaders to steer businesses into a successful and sustainable future. I took into account not only the input from my industry leaders, but also input from existing literature as well as global business developments.

Future Perspectives of Business in the 21st Century (in Relation to Existing Literature)

With dramatic change now a clear feature of business, leaders would be well advised to become aware of and explore the mental models that shape their actions. Leaders are advised to see the new "writing on the wall" in the business context. In order to obtain a picture of how the winning organisation will look in the future, an academic named Markovic concluded that successful companies in the future will be those that are wise enough to harness the full potential of the entire organisation in the ever-changing business environment.[60] The winners are the ones who are most responsive to challenges and quicker to create and effectively exploit evolving opportunities. More effectual mental models, frameworks of understanding and the ability to withstand uncertainty and manage rapid change, are vital. Prevailing business leaders should serve as champions and custodians of change.[61]

Markovic highlighted the following critical business factors that could signify a winning organisation in the new era:

- Firstly, the importance of *continuous learning* in what will become ever more a knowledge economy, with competitive advantage inevitably tied to appropriate questioning, understanding and innovation, at both an individual and a collective level.

- Secondly, the acquisition of *market-related information* and its dissemination throughout the business. Markovic indicated that up to 80% of US businesses fail within their first year, almost exclusively as a result of their inability to fully understand their markets.

- Thirdly, *selecting appropriate staff*. Markovic proposes three significant issues regarding human capital, that they need to demonstrate:

  i)   early ability
  ii) qualifications and knowledge acquired through education
  iii) skills, competencies, and expertise acquired through both on-the-job and off-the-job training.

Werhane, a renowned scholar and writer in Systems Thinking, argues that in the new era, business leaders will have to take a moral, systems-thinking approach because some of the business parts relate to humanity issues or human concerns.[62] (The business leaders in my study raised the importance of considering human issues within their broader leadership thinking). Using a systems approach, I perceive that organisations are embedded in much larger political, economic, legal, cultural systems, and even global systems, which make for occasional unpredictability. Systems are connected in ways that could be micro (small, self-contained with few interconnections) or macro (large, complex, consisting of a number of interconnections).Furthermore, complex global systems can make the system unpredictable sometimes.

Margaret Wheatley, who is a voice of authority in theories of management ,introduced a theme of unpredictability from the angle of *unpredictable* chaos. Wheatley perceives the universe as inherently orderly but as a living system. The universe seeks to create and re-create itself in order to evolve and keep on reaching "orderliness and capacity", referring to this as "chaos that contains order".[63]Nel and Beudeker similarly believe that the 21st century will be chaotic and therefore disruptive to what has been the previously established order and that this is necessary for businesses, as living systems, to continuously evolve.

To deal more comfortably with the ongoing turbulence they envision, these theorists recommend openness, willingness to let go of old ways of seeing the world, including the business world, and being prepared for a total paradigm shift. This will encourage business to venture into important new territories and create structural and behavioural changes so as to re-establish a sense of order. The organisation, as a living organism, will reorganise its form to create another "being" which is better suited to the new changed environment. As Wheatley says, the system's disintegration does not signal its death but rather demonstrates its ability to re-create itself. For leaders in the 21st century, it would be important to understand how newness evolves and that disorder can be a source of a new order. We should, therefore, accept a "new science thinking" that studies living organisms as organs of life, and see *"life as life"*,[64] moving away from a mechanistic point of view. Organisational theorists now speak of organic structures, fluid structures, seamless organisations, and learning organisations, indicating an acceptance of the truth in Wheatley's insights that organisations are truly living systems with the same capacity to evolve and grow, which is inherent in all forms of life.

Wheatley further describes the new era as having networks and interconnected systems, where a slight change in one part of the system often results in unavoidable changes in other parts and may even have ripple effects where far away parts are impacted. In this highly sensitive system, even minimal actions can blow up into massive disruptions and chaos. Nevertheless, it is also a world that seeks order. When chaos erupts, it not only disintegrates the current structure, and also creates the conditions for a new order to emerge.

With this in mind, the concept of organisational structure/design of the 21st century will be briefly discussed scholastically because it featured in the mental models and was noted among the remarkable challenges that business leaders are facing in this new global era.

Organizational Design for the 21stcentury

The overriding assumption in the multitude of theories/approaches to organisational evolution is that success is closely linked with organizational dynamics, structures, levels of bureaucracy, and division of labour, etc. In addition, organizational structure and design, as well as organizational behaviour, has a reciprocal influence.

My aim here is not to discuss design or structural issues but to explore the implication of these when a business lacks the ability to be sufficiently nimble and flexible. These are critical attributes when there is a need to act or react promptly to side-step disastrous circumstances or deal with unavoidable turbulence dictated to it by the external environment within which it operates.

For business in general, the transition into the 21st century heralded pressure for enhanced speed in all operations and processes, heightened flexibility and decisiveness, even in the absence of complete information, as well as foresight and proactivity. Thus, it becomes imperative that business leaders are able to design structures which will accommodate these requirements for nimble functioning when the demand arises.

Drucker postulated that in the new era, organisational structures would bear little resemblance to previous hierarchal designs and would rather be knowledge or information-based. He suggested that an information-based organization would call for far more specialists than a command and control company. Goold and Campbell concluded that most organizational structures were shaped more by politics than policies.[65]My own viewpoint is that informal authority is gaining traction in a great many corporates and there is significantly less reliance on formal structures by business leaders, especially when dealing with the realities of an unstable operating environment and when taking critical decisions.

The speed with which people, whether inside or outside a business, are able to access key information is challenging old bureaucratic norms in terms of how quickly decisions can be made in the face of new knowledge. Progressive organisations are realising the benefit of adopting models that enable informal information processing and decision-making wherever the need arises for business effectiveness. Wheatley says: "innovation is fostered by new data gathered from new connections; from insights established through paths into other disciplines or places; from active, collegial networks and fluid, open boundaries and structures.[66]

Some of the leaders in my study related how they sometimes had to make urgent trips or even impromptu conference calls to other countries to gather data to enable them to make rapid decisions. This has become a common occurrence amongst business leaders, especially those leading multinationals. The electronic availability of instant real-time information can differentiate between an effective and an ineffective organisation, often achieved through a network-based structure across several countries. My leaders stressed this as a critical aspect of efficiency and effectiveness in business today and, increasingly so, in the future. International networks or transnational structures also facilitate access to required competencies. The entire world will be used as a platform for progressively gaining skills, knowledge and expertise, whether it's to achieve specific project short-term objectives or even on a longer-term basis; we see this in many businesses sourcing critical skills across the globe for particular assignments.[67]In this study, business leaders raised the issue of critical skills shortage which pushes them to use the entire global network to access the critical skills at any given time as per need.

As the international business context becomes increasingly complex, diverse, and dynamic, organizations will structure themselves around exploiting opportunities for international networking, collaboration and as a result, business competitiveness will be gauged through the capacity for business to become more transnational.[68]

The Business Culture of the 21stCentury

Multiculturism is the reality of the 21st century. The world is evolving in intricate ways, and although people might immediately think of technological difference, the people differences are equally dramatic.[69]In business, the concept of culture has gained prominence as we have experienced the momentum created by the workplace having become a space where people of different cultural backgrounds are increasingly interacting. Many authors seem to refer to the concept of culture as simply a way of doing things or a way in which individuals share meanings and common ways of viewing events and objects.[70]However, when speaking from a business perspective, culture generally refers to the way in which things are done within an organization and what people encounter as the touch and feel during their personal experiences.

For South African businesses, the challenge will be to understand and adapt to the different cultural norms they are being exposed to. Currently, global culture is largely Western because Western countries dominate the global economy, and it is characterised by freedom of choice, individual rights and competition.[71]However, this may change over time and, certainly, SA businesspeople are increasingly interacting with additional global players. Undoubtedly, the role of culture in new global definitions of work will become more evident as the century unfolds. In his research, Hofstede explored the characteristics and roles of culture in the workplace. He established five dimensions that relate to work and behaviour and he compared these across a range of countries to examine the differences and similarities. His conclusion was that some dimensions seem more effective in certain cultures than in others and it would therefore be important for businesspeople to note that what may work well in one culture may not work as well, or even at all, in another.[72]As businesses seek to entrench themselves within global networks and as they increasing deal with multinationals, this reality will have major implications. It is my opinion that the greatest need is for openness to new thinking and new approaches to business and for making better use of the benefits of cultural diversity. Business will be impacted by the influx of millennials and centennials into the labour market and will need to reconsider itself and to ensure cultures that appeal to dynamic new generations.

What can be concluded as true is that "culture matters and will matter more and more in the 21st century."[73]

Given the nature of the study and the calibre of the industry leaders who partook in it, the discussion would not be complete without looking into aspects of leadership of the 21st century. The leaders also highlighted the theme of leading and experiences thereof in the new era.

Chapter Conclusion

For South Africa, business seems to be facing challenges from internal and external factors, both of which shape the thinking and actions of business leaders. The key points of the narratives of the business leaders provided an indication of their current experiences and lenses through which they saw business in South Africa and the globe, as well as how they envisaged the business of the 21st century. Their thinking served as basis for the provision of a guideline or framework for leading business in the 21st century.

5

IMPLICATIONS FOR GLOBAL BUSINESS LEADERSHIP IN THE 21ST CENTURY

IT IS BECOMING more and more evident that globalisation is not a straightforward, orderly process. There is inevitably a certain level of uncertainty and uncontrollability. Based on this reality, authors such as Meyer and Boninelli have emphasised that globalisation is fragile.[74] The World Economic Forum (WEF) in 2002 concurred with this viewpoint, when the theme of discussion was Leadership in Fragile Times. The Forum acknowledged that the world's biggest economies, as well as many of those currently emerging, had slowed simultaneously, thereby creating precarious prospects. It was realised that the future of globalisation would "lie firmly in the hands of social, political, and business leaders; that the process of globalisation was not a spontaneous, perpetual, self-actualising, and self-fuelling process but that it would be directed and powered by these leaders". (World Economic Forum, 2002).

When launching the South African National Development Plan in 2012, the then Minister in the Presidency, Trevor Manuel, echoed these sentiments:

The global economy is changing, with a rising share of production and wealth generation occurring in developing

73

countries in general and Asia in particular. Globalisation will continue apace with both risks and opportunities for all countries. Countries that position themselves to take advantage of the opportunities while protecting their economies (and the poor) from risks will do better over the next two decades…The world is changing at breath-taking speed…A failure to act will not just see us being left behind. It will also confine future generations to poverty and hopelessness.[75]

It will be incumbent on leaders, therefore, to carve out and spearhead the direction of globalisation. Both developed and still developing world economies will certainly have a role to play in discussions at this level and will help to realise the ultimate goals of the WEF. Even as South Africa engages in business forum explorations, such as the G20 and B20, its business leaders need to become a committed and cohesive force devoted to shaping the future of globalisation. In the specific case of South Africa, both business and government leaders have to bear this in mind all the time as we still try to establish our footprint on these global platforms.

In the perception of those industry leaders I spoke with, whilst designing strategic imperatives that will enable not only growth at a local level but also competition in a broader sphere, there is an increasing awareness of the global perspective and the need for South Africa to rise to the challenging setting in. Meyer and Boninelli clearly stress the need for leaders to realise the significance of their actions and reactions in shaping the future of the economy, both nationally and globally.[76]Their key message revolves around the encompassing responsibilities of leadership in terms of social, cultural, organisational, spiritual and moral issues. Overall, leaders in my study felt it was particularly important for leadership to be authentic, especially as corruption seemed to be rife in both government and private sectors, to avoid unscrupulous practices that were pulling the country backwards.

They also believed it was of great benefit that the entire African continent was now beginning to become involved in global platforms.

The Effective/Successful Global Leader

Much has been written regarding business leadership from a theoretical standpoint, including by Blanchard[77] (known for situational leadership),and Blake and Mouton[78](known for designing the managerial grid), as well as many others. What is clearly required, over and above what already exists, is a better understanding of the implications of leadership in a modern economy, given world developments and crises that promise ongoing turbulence which will doubtless result in fundamental changes in the workplace. Literature is already full of unsettling descriptions of the challenges ahead for business leaders, with words such as "volatile", "multidimensional", and "unprecedented" being used.[79]In other writings, the descriptors include "unpredictable", "contradictory", "deep" and so on.[80]Industry leaders in this study agreed that these emotive expressions portrayed the reality business was living with and that yesterday's solutions will be hopelessly inadequate, given the dynamics of a highly uncertain 21st century.

Examples of complexity and challenges that were raised by the industry leaders included, amongst others, the question of international competition, turnaround time, offering complete solutions to clients' shortages of skilled employees, and the volatile rand.

Successful global leaders need to be able to both recognise and manage paradox within complex and chaotic scenarios .Letting go of either/or mentality would be just one of their essential mindset shifts. Successful leaders are able to shift calculatedly when a situation calls for a mindset shift. They must demonstrate the mental agility[81]to deal effectively with perplexing and contradictory situations. In dissecting the concept of leadership in this era of complexity, theorists posit that effective leadership is going to require maintaining multiple points of stability within an environmental context of flux, in order to facilitate deliberate and appropriate direction amidst apparent chaos.[82]There is a call for leaders to realize the significance of their actions and reactions in shaping the future of our economy, both nationally and globally.[83]

Similarly, Veldsman notes that sustainability is largely a leadership responsibility particularly in the era of globalism. Although he is cautious about the specific competencies required of leaders, Veldsman suggests that leadership should match the required levels of complexity inherent in that portfolio of the leader. In addition, he concludes that the challenges identified do not exist or function in silos but impact and reinforce one another.[84]

Nel and Beudeker are of the opinion that the first two decades of the new millennium may see one of the greatest shifts ever experienced by modern humanity because this revolution is being driven by a combination of hard as well as soft factors. The hard factors are those that are technological and the soft factors are human.[85]They see these factors as drivers of economic transformation at a political and social level.

The latest approach to the concept of leadership that seems to be emerging along with the concept of sustainability is that of transcendental leadership. As a scholar, Verwey argued that for leadership to find meaning, it must be value-based and spiritual. Transformational leadership should also be based on particular values and ethics, such as collaboration and service orientation. Thus, leadership is expressed from a three-dimensional perspective: transactional, transformational, and transcendental. The premise of this three-dimensional approach seems to suggest that the role of leadership concerns *doing things right while doing the right thing.*

My belief is that future leadership will embrace insights and actions from transactional, transformation, and transcendental frameworks and will utilise these appropriately, depending on the contexts within which they find themselves, both locally and globally. Transcendental leadership refers more to the promotion of intrinsic values and spirituality and I feel these will become increasingly more important for expression in this 21st century. I am in support of the thinking that given the speed, dynamism and complexity of the 21st century, even this concept of transcendental leadership is changing, even though its prominence is recent relative to the two concepts of transactional and transformational leadership. It is already changing in shape, shade, character and meaning given the speed at which things are changing and the complexity we are seeing in the world now .Leaders of today are experiencing challenges that call for what Nel and Beudeker to as "the leadership revolution".[86]Another writer says that new leadership DNA is required with sharper traits, behaviour, approaches, practices, and guidelines that would be more fitting to the challenges of the 21st century.[87]

Current leaders need to explicitly focus not only on leading others, but also on leading themselves, that is becoming truly authentic. Winning leaders will be those showing reliability, resilience and the capacity to continually adapt to circumstances, whilst retaining integrity, being consistently aligned with their own morals and values.

The diagram below depicts the calibre of leadership that would probably achieve greater success in aligning South Africa with the global front. My personal views (as informed by theoretical and practical experience) are that the dynamics and complexity of leadership in this century of sustainability and globalisation have begun redefining the substance of what successful leadership is about. Global leadership means a leader needs to operate at multiple levels at any particular circumstance in the life of an organisation. It has become about simultaneously juggling balls that may have shades, weights and elements that cross several domains, therefore testing different aspects of leadership at once. In today's times, successful leaders tend to be those that can demonstrate this level of elasticity whilst not dropping any of these balls and remaining fluid but sustainable in profits and maintaining exposure to global intelligence. With the business world becoming open and global, networks and global organisations mean that leadership is also about successfully leading self, others, teams and organisations across the continent and the globe, with all the dynamics of building relations and attaining greater heights of competitiveness. Multifaceted leadership has become the norm and has somewhat become the base for determining success in the 21st century of globalisation and growth.

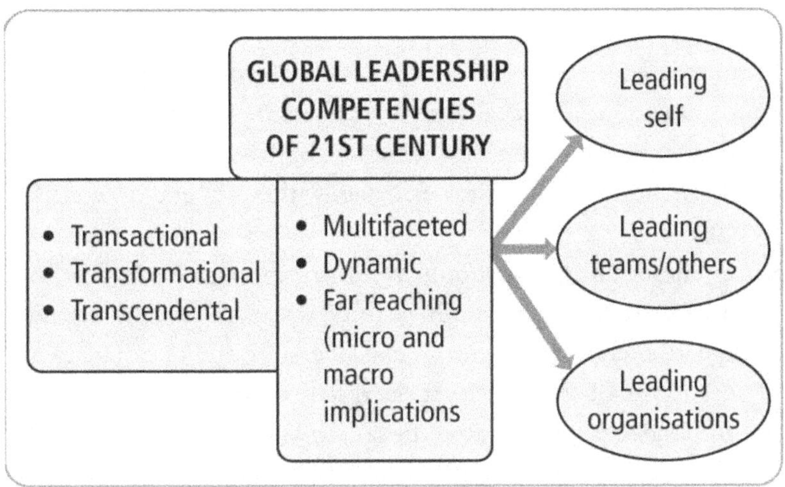

Figure 11: The Leadership dynamic of the 21st century

In accordance with the leadership aspects as depicted in the diagram above, the business leaders' mental models suggested several things:

1. They experience challenge as leaders of business where the objectives are to be gainful (profitable) but also to *lead others or even themselves* competitively.

2. Their leadership skills are stretched at all three levels, i.e. *transactional, transformation* and even *transcendental.*

3. Another key challenge expressed by the business leaders was that in leading themselves and others, they are expected to demonstrate the leadership skill of *balancing humanity, operational aspects, and overall business mindedness,* especially for the black leaders who are expected to satisfy both shareholder expectations and the expectations of their black employees who look up to them as messiahs who can change their working conditions.

4. On a global front, the business leaders face challenges as they venture into the African continent, as well as the international space as global players. They have to quickly adapt and learn

other ways of conducting business, cultural dynamics, competency and skills dynamics, business growth and competition. The challenge is characterized by the reality that they have to remain relevant both internationally and domestically – all this occurring within an era of constant change.

5.   Domestically ,the government leadership, business leaders, and organized labour cannot afford to push totally separate agendas while the country's challenges are still perforated with the issues of the first layer (as discussed in an earlier chapter) and leaders try to position the country's economy to handle the dynamics of the second (globalization) and third layers (21st century).What emerged from the mental models was that the lack of effective dialogue between the three organs of the South African economy is stifling the economy of the country and its progress. It not only affects the economics of the country domestically, but also in the country's offshore activities by compromising our competitiveness globally. Given the reality that South Africa is in a transitional state and is still riddled with the three-layered challenge of improving the economy, the calibre of leadership, as well as their mindsets, remains critical in many ways. This was indicated in the mental models of the participant business leaders whose views seemed to suggest that the business of today calls for a more vigilant, vibrant and competitive mindset. The mental models emerged as suggestive of a new type of thinking by business leaders in order to survive the challenges of the 21st century – at a transactional, transformational and transcendental level.

6.   Once more, on a domestic front, their competencies are challenged by having to position their businesses for profitability within a weakening economy due to various factors, given that South Africa is still a growing democracy. For example, this is evident in their narratives as they referred

to the issues of infrastructure, skills shortages, lowered productivity levels, and labour issues, amongst others.

In closing, business leaders need to comprehend the business environment in its totality at both local and global levels – *even if they are not running global businesses*. Local businesses will be impacted by global trends and dynamics, so leaders have to keep an eye on the bigger picture at all times.

SA Business Conclusions

In view of the overall information, starting from the input or stories told by the participant business leaders, to the literature, and to developments regarding the government undertakings on the National Development Plan, to what is generally known from the media and news, we cannot deny that South Africa has come a long way in opening up avenues for business. However, to date, South African businesses remain shadowed by the challenges of having to close the gaps left by the legacy of apartheid.

On a global scale, the market is putting its own pressure on South African leaders to steer business in the right direction at a pace that matches the speed at which globalisation is unfolding worldwide. Opportunities come up, but equally so do the potential threats and risks that could impact the South African economy badly if not carefully managed.

On the home front, the country has some housecleaning to do before we can confidently enter the world stage as a strong economy, even though we are a member of the BRICS and are slowly convincing the world that we have the potential of being an economic gateway to Africa alongside Nigeria.

Regarding the country's leadership in both business and government, we have to acknowledge that we have our own share of shortcomings. For example, as a result of issues of corruption and crime within business and governmental sectors, the economy is lagging. Relationships between government and business are also admittedly lacking trust and partnership. From a cultural perspective and the way we are doing things, we need to mend our ways and instil a culture of morality, uphold high ethical standards, and focus on humanity issues in order to create fertile ground for the successful implementation of the NDP, amongst other imperatives in this century. President Cyril Ramaphosa often reiterates the importance of instilling a culture of morality across government entities and business to curb the high level of corruption that is crippling our steps towards the rollout of the NDP.

From a leadership perspective, as our leaders demonstrate mastery of the key dimensions of transactional and transformation leadership, the time has come to focus on transcendental leadership, where business places more focus on issues of humanity and environmental sustainability. In the words of our former president, Nelson Mandela, leaders need to invoke high levels of conscience as citizens of the country, that is, invoke "the RDP of the soul" and save humanity. The notion of transcendental leadership is still relatively new in the literature, but it must be given serious consideration if our leaders are to demonstrate the capacity to lead South Africa to sustainability for generations to come.

Even though the concept of global warming did not necessarily feature in the mental models of the business leaders, it is no doubt that this will form part of the challenges in the next decade or two as the globe becomes more pressed with this aspect. In a study conducted by the CSIR, the main researcher, Dr Bob Scholes, said South Africa was warming up faster than the global average as a result of climate change, and this was posing a threat to our ecosystems as well as our ability to create food and to develop socially. Scholes says that South Africa's policies need to seriously address the issue of global warming. In a survey conducted by Deloitte around 2017, even millennials regarded issues around climate change as amongst the top five factors of importance, especially within emerging markets. Thus, given the reality that it is these young workers who will dominate the world of work in this 21st century, these are the challenges they will have to be equipped to deal with. Exposing them to these challenges as future leaders will only serve to better the country in this time of multiple complexities.

Both government and business face a challenge of incorporating this challenge of global warming in the broader sphere of challenges of the 21st century. Sustainability (particularly environmental) demands that this issue be looked into with more vigour and determination to minimize the more negative consequences of climate change. It has become a pressing issue of the 21st century and will pose a challenge for South Africa as the country endeavours to play a competitive or sustainable role in the globe.

In conclusion, South Africa is in an era of challenges requiring shifts in thinking and doing, also influenced by the entire global ecosystem. These challenges seem to be dressed in quite bold gear that spells out a need for some fundamental and bold shifts in our approach for the sake of our economy going into the 21st century. Business, government and labour leadership are called upon to rise to these challenges through a genuine partnership and mindset.

For business, in particular, the context is changing and the boundaries of business are becoming blurred, or disappearing altogether, and interconnectedness has spread worldwide and continues to grow. This seems to be setting businesses up to move into survival mode, since some will undoubtedly have the resilience to endure, while others will simply sink into the morass and disappear.

With the 21st century challenges fast galloping into our business and economic space, business in South Africa cannot deny the emergence of another character of leadership. What emerged from this study was that business leaders acknowledged that certain key perspectives were required to adequately meet the dynamism of the 21st century. Furthermore, the influence of sustainability as a management paradigm came sharply into focus – sustainability is undeniably becoming the new thinking.

For South Africa, the question that comes along with the concept of an SMO (sustainable management organisation) is how to address the challenges of the apartheid legacy. Whilst South African business seeks to rise to the challenges of instilling a sustainable management philosophical approach, the local challenges related to the previous regime still need dire attention and resources. Our philosophical frameworks have to measure up to sustainability in the 21t century. During the study, the industry captains admitted to the need for mental models to also form cornerstones to these frameworks that are likely to measure up to the dynamism of the 21st century whilst feeding the call for sustainable management.

Below are some of the key perspectives from the mental models of business leaders. These perspectives are seen to feed into the concept of sustainable management. The main attempt was to find a way of consolidating a comprehensive framework encompassing the:

- critical elements of the 21st century;
- the concept of the SMO as possibly replacing or enriching the HIO (high involvement organisation); and
- the current scenario of South Africa with its three-layered challenges.

A shared perspective from those leaders who participated in my study was that South Africa must elevate itself to global levels by gaining presence and recognition within the world as a whole. While mindful of the current challenges, both domestically and globally, business leaders appear positive, even while acknowledging that the 21st century calls for a sharper and more vigorous approach.

At a macro, or external level, the challenges noted above, as South Africa moves further into the 21st century, may well ultimately require a closer look at national policies, for example, the new dispensation of a tripartite system consisting of the ANC, the workers, and the socialists. The implications for business of this evolution must receive attention from all those affected. In addition, the downgrading of the SA economy by the World Bank deserves some serious focus regarding emerging constraints, especially from a cost-benefit perspective and the overall expense of doing business.

At a micro, or internal level, the critical skills shortage and the dire need for skills development call for more high-pitched decisions regarding structural arrangements, particularly as old hierarchal structures are coming into question with the movement into increasing global competitiveness.

The opinions of my study participants also illustrate the components of political, economic, and technological unpredictability which will inevitably become part of business reality

Nevertheless, a sustainable organization was envisioned as clearly possible, given the ability to deliberately become aware of circumstances and to rethink and realign appropriately.

Without doubt, the days when "the business of business is business" are over. Political, social, and international aspects have become an essential component of the business agenda, both within the country and outside its borders. My question is: *Are these mental models telling a story with regard to the management evolution and are these mental models also indicating that a new management reset is here?*

Indeed, I am led to believe that previous business management theories no longer suffice in this era of unprecedented uncertainty and turbulence. What stands out for me is that the thinking of those leaders I spoke with was influenced by the rationale of HIOs. There are still some traces of COO (command and control organisations) doctrines, evidenced through their need to maintain control and command through formal structures, although these were merely traces. Their inclination is definitely leaning towards more HIO and SMO principles.

The leaders I interviewed thought that the country was generally moving towards the eradication of overt discrimination.

They were positive about the opportunities offered by globalisation, possibilities of venturing into multinational ventures or partnerships and of easier access to skills and technology. They felt South Africa was starting to play a meaningful role not only in the African Union but also in the European Union. They saw it as a major benefit that SA companies were venturing into Africa, for example in telecommunications.

The downside was the concern that the distant relationship with government was hampering economic progress. Although dialogue has been initiated regarding the rollout of the NDP, they were worried that there was no clarity as to who would or should drive this process.

Finally, sustainability was a crucial topic as the leaders acknowledged the call for business to develop more of a conscience about the environment in general and in the specific issues of humanity.

How might these scenarios be united to construct an inclusive framework for guidance towards creating profitable SMOs?

The diagram below captures the concept of SMOs from these three logical perspectives:

The top part shows how management philosophies have evolved from COOs into HIOs and even SMOs. However, what we see in organisations of the day is that some elements of the COO and HIO are still prevalent. This implies that with the emergence of the needs for SMOs, we can ask whether this management paradigm is replacing the HIO or improving it by introducing insights of the SMO, especially with regards to sustainability.

The middle part of the diagram highlights the emergence of the 21st century which comes along with these key challenges: high complexity, speed, ambiguity, and competitiveness. The 21st century is also characterized by the notion of sustainability, which embraces value creation and humanity.

The bottom part incorporates the unique case of South African where the economy navigates these challenges while still grappling with the remnants of the old discriminatory era. This refers to the framework that was introduced in an earlier chapter in discussing the three-layered complexity of the South African economy.

The challenge of business is therefore to find operational frameworks of how to operate business within this context and to face the many challenges of the 21st century.

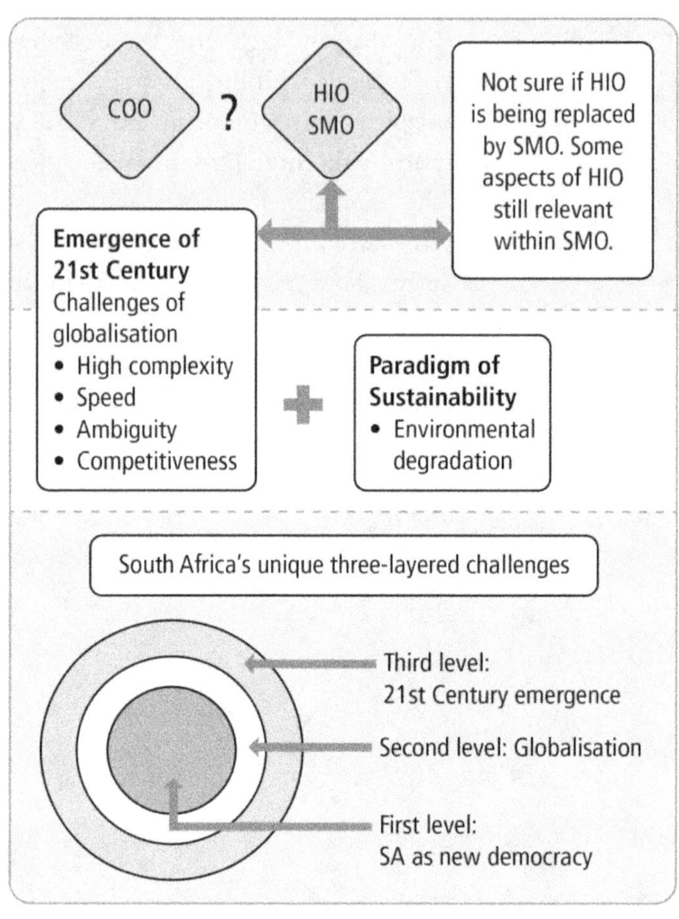

Figure 12: Inclusive framework for SMOs

6

CONCLUSIONS AND RECOMMENDATIONS

GIVEN THE INPUT of the business leaders and the perspectives they shared with me, the available literature, and current South African government undertakings, particularly the NDP, it cannot be denied that the country has come a long way in terms of opening up avenues for business. However, to date, businesses need to close the many gaps lingering in the shadows of apartheid. In addition, there remains the danger of excessive focus on shorter-term issues and reluctance to engage with bigger uncertainties, even though these are likely to ultimately be of more importance.

The global market is pressuring South African leaders to steer business in the right direction at a speed befitting the worldwide pace of globalisation. Certainly, there are exciting opportunities, but the potential risks need to be faced and managed if the economy is not to be negatively impacted. This includes some housecleaning measures before South Africa can confidently step onto the world stage as a strong economy.

As a whole, the country needs to address corruption and crime, especially within business and government, to support economic development. A culture of morality and authenticity must be cultivated, with an appropriate focus on human factors.

Leaders need to model the key dimensions of transactional and transformational leadership. In addition, attention must be paid to transcendental leadership approaches, to ensure sufficient emphasis is placed on issues of humanity and environmental sustainability. Although the notion of transcendental leadership is still relatively new in the literature, it is imperative that it be given serious consideration if the country is to achieve sustainability for generations yet to come.

What was revealed in this study was that sustainability was of less importance than the immediate concerns of those leaders I interviewed, i.e. that of keeping their businesses afloat in the short to medium term. This was in spite of expressing some awareness of the need for contributing to a longer-term sustainable future. The mental models revealed that the thinking is there, albeit to a lesser extent than more immediate concerns of profitability.

Positioning their businesses on a global scale appeared to be on their boardroom agendas, along with, to some extent, applicable political concerns. However, since these leaders identified with the chaos, paradox and fierce competitiveness ahead, it is my belief that sustainability will increasingly become a relevant issue on business agendas.

In view of the voice of South African business and current mental models, what should form part of thinking for business going forward?

- Closing the gaps left by the legacy of apartheid still remains a huge challenge for South Africa, and business cannot afford not to prioritize this responsibility.
- Taking a consistent bigger picture and longer-term perspective, both within business and government, to avoid focusing only on short terms gains, would be critical for sustainability within the country.
- Given that millennials and centennials will dominate the world of work in this 21st century, we need to be more diligently equipping them for the challenges ahead.

- We need to acknowledge and redress our shortcomings, such as corruption, and open up authentic dialogue between business and government to instil a culture of morality and humanity that will facilitate the successful implementation of the NDP, amongst other imperatives.

- On a global scale, markets are pressuring the country's leaders to steer business in a direction and at a pace commensurate with the rapid unfolding of globalisation. This requires vigilance to spot emerging opportunities, but also to identify potential threats that could negatively impact the economy if not carefully managed.

- Some housecleaning will be necessary on the home front before being able to confidently enter the world stage as a strong economy and to convince the world we have the potential of sitting alongside Nigeria as an economic gateway to the African continent.

- From a leadership perspective, the time has come to focus more on transcendental leadership, where business places emphasis on human and environmental sustainability. The notion of transcendental leadership may be relatively new in literature but must be given serious consideration if our leaders are to demonstrate the capacity to lead South Africa to sustainability for generations to come.

- Of concern was the observation that global warming did not specifically feature as a priority challenge to business. There is nevertheless no doubt that this will find its way into agendas shortly, particularly as this issue gains global importance. South Africa is warming faster than the world average, thereby posing a threat to our ecosystems and to food production. Sustainability, particularly environmental, demands that this issue be looked into with more intent to minimise the unfavourable consequences of climate change.

Contributions of the Study

The field of industrial/organisational psychology primarily depends on research for drawing conclusions that link real-world problems to scientific understanding. Organisational psychology "stretches itself beyond the physical constraints and boundaries of workspaces because the factors that influence the work behaviour are not exclusively found in a work setting.[88]Leaders of organisations acknowledge that events occurring outside of work settings may influence business. Thus, my motivation was to get the voice of leaders on how they see the road ahead for South African business in the 21st century.

The evolution of management theories fundamentally affects mental models, which in turn shape thinking and behaviour, particularly those of business leaders. External environmental forces must be factored into their strategies for organisational success to be enabled.

In exploring the mental models of business in South Africa, the study has revealed what underlies the thinking of business leaders as they face challenges of today. Put differently, the study has identified the thinking of business within a particular context, and thereby packaged current challenges into identifiable business terms.

Timing of the Study

I believe my study has relevance because, more than 25 years into democracy, South Africa has witnessed changes on political, social, and to some extent, economic fronts. The business fraternity has had to adapt and align itself to changes within the country, as well as to broader national and international trends, and in my view, appropriately so given the tripartite economic system in South Africa. There is little doubt that there are major challenges ahead, including complexities that appear to be threatening not only the foundations of business as it has been experienced previously, but also government as well. These complexities are going to have to be recognised and tackled if the country's economic stance is to improve.

Despite strides having been made, there are unanswered questions:

- Can South African business, government and labour genuinely join forces to ensure a sustainable future for everyone, given that the issues of business survival, global competitiveness, and the ability to manage uncertainties have become paramount for leaders, notwithstanding the fact that the country still grapples with more bread and butter issues?
- Are new business practices emerging rapidly enough to deal with a global world of endless and unpredictable surprise where we never know what we will hear when we turn on the news.
- Is the issue of sustainability that is emerging whispering a paradigm shift for business? Are we positioning ourselves for this probability? Given the reality of sustainability and the 21st-century theme of speed, complexity, and paradox, is business readying itself for new models of effective leadership, business policies, practices and competitiveness?

≈

ABOUT THE AUTHOR

Dr Thandiwe Gama is an executive coach, author and registered Industrial & Organisational Psychologist. She holds a PhD in Industrial Psychology from the University of Johannesburg.

Thandiwe's field of specialty has been in organisational development and change management. In the last few years, her work has focused on executive coaching, with an emphasis on performance and personal alignment.

This book emerged from her extensive experience in business and consulting and her research into future trends in both small and large businesses.

Email: tgama@mweb.co.za
Twitter: @DrThandiwe
Linkedin: Dr Thandiwe Gama

ENDORSEMENTS

THANDIWE'S BOOK is thought-provoking and most timely in the current context of South Africa as we grapple with economic uncertainty and social issues such as unemployment and poverty. She gained my attention in her introduction, when she asks us: *Mzansi, what are you seeing in this dawn of the 21st century?* The key focus of the book is sharing her research findings on the perspectives of South African CEOs to answer this question. Through a combination of leadership theory and the voices of these CEOs, I appreciated the graphic picture she paints of the complexity of the challenges facing business, both locally and in the global context. Thandiwe uses her research to make a persuasive case for sustainable leadership, which is primarily in its nascent phase in South Africa. What stands out is her emphasis on the dire need for collaboration between business, government and organised labour to find a common path forward to grow our economy <u>and</u> to address the social concerns and the environmental challenges facing us. Yet she acknowledges the difficulties in getting this form of collaboration to occur.

Nonetheless, Thandiwe rightly argues that business can no longer afford to be just about business. She calls business leaders to action – to embrace sustainable leadership in the true sense through adopting leadership that engenders a conscience, responsibility and morality beyond a focus on short-term profits. A meaningful framework is then provided to guide leaders in the critical thinking and strategizing required to make this happen. This book is essential reading for leaders who care about the future of our country and who want to make a sustainable difference.

—Dr Kathy Bennett, Leadership Coach & Adjunct Faculty
Member, University of Stellenbosch

THIS BOOK IS RELEVANT to leaders, managers, individuals and practitioners who have vested interests in ensuring that business becomes successful and South Africa flourish as a country. The complex changes in and outside the organisations are inevitable and will continue, demanding different paradigms and mental models. The past models are obsolete and call for a diverse and new perspective. All the key stakeholders such as business, government, labour and society need to take responsibility and accountability and come up with new ideas and solutions to resolve the matter. In the process, they need to be mindful of the need to generate maximum profits while taking care of the people and planet to benefit the next generations

The themes identified in this book provide insights into some of the priority areas to consider in order to bring about lasting changes, including globalisation, competitiveness, knowledge management and information sharing, technological advancement and the use of social networks, customer-focused turnaround time, solution-driven thinking, youth empowerment and authentic leadership. To effectively deal with the changes, there is a need to leverage the internal strengths of the individual and collective power of the organisation to ensure success. The future of our country and business starts now with adequate engagements, planning and implementation of programmes that are sustainable. By encouraging diverse perspectives, new and unique ideas arise that can help to address the challenges in business and society."

—Sylvia Baloyi, Industrial Psychologist, Transition Coach and
Director at Lehlogonolo HR Consulting

WITH THE GOVERNMENT'S continued emphasis on growing the economy and creating opportunities for foreign investors, South African businesses are progressively becoming significant players in the international economy.

Business in the 21st Century is an incisive book that provides helpful insights about the role of leadership in driving transformation and sustainability strategies in this 21stcentury. Backed by solid research, the author amalgamates perspectives from South Africa's top business leaders and illuminates the risks and challenges as well as the enormous talent and innovation opportunities that the new era presents. As you read this book you will get an insightful view about thought leadership and process of balancing the country's business capabilities with realities of a rapidly changing world and increasing global competitiveness.

Dr Gama is one of the masters of business transformation, having spent two decades in corporate leadership, consulting and technology services industries. She turned her back on the lucrative corporate career to pursue her own dreams. With deep intellect and humility, she changed her course of life and turned into a successful entrepreneur. She presents *Business in the 21st Century* with a deeply rooted understanding of how leveraging the talent, innovation and growing market opportunities is important for the survival of business today.

I have benefited from her insights and recommend this book for any individual who is forward looking and keen to revive and sustain their business.

A must-read for business executives and prospective entrepreneurs.

—Zime Hlatshwayo, Executive Director, Quandophase Investments

BIBLIOGRAPHY

Adonis, M. and van Wyk, R. (2012). The influence of Market
Orientation, Flexibility and Job Service on Corporate
Entrepreneurship. *International Business & Economics Research
Journal*, 11 (5).

Ajzen, I. (2001). Nature and operation of attitudes. *Annual Review of
Psychology,* 52, 27-58.

Barr, P.S., Stimpert, J.L. & Huff, A.S. (1992). Cognitive change,
strategic action and organizational renewal. *Strategic Management
Journal*, 13, 15-36.

Baskin, J. (2006). *Value, values and sustainability: Corporate responsibility
in emerging market companies.* Available at
http://ssm.com/abstract=1094573.

Bathembu, C. (2010). *South Africa Pulls together: Zuma.* Accessed on
2011-07-20.Available from
http://www.sa.info/news/international.

Beinart, W. (2001). *Twentieth century South Africa* (2nd ed.). Oxford:
Oxford University Press.

Bennis, W. and Mische, M. (1995). The 21st-century organisation:
Re-inventing through re-engineering. San Diego: Pfeiffer & Co.

Benvenista, G. (1994). The twenty-first century organisation:
Analyzing current trends, imagining the future. San Francisco,
CA: Jossey-Bass Publishers.

Bhagat, S.R., Segovis, C.J., & Nelson, A.T.(2012). *Work stress and
coping in the era of globalisation.* New York: Routledge Taylor and
Francis Group.

Blake, R. & Mouton, J. (1985). *The Managerial Grid III: The Key to
Leadership Excellence.* Houston: Gulf Publishing Co.

Blanchard, K. (1994). *The one-minute manager.* London: Harper
Collins.

Cho, C.H., Meyer, D.M. & Roberts, R.W. (2006). Corporate
political strategy:An examination of the relation between

political expenditures, environmental performance and environmental disclosure. *Journal of Business Ethics*, 67(2), 139-154.

Coetzee, J. (2012). *The social contract with business*. Bloomington, IS: Xlibris Corporation Publishing.

Cohen, E. (2008).Welcome to the new global frontier. *T AND D, 62*(2),www.wbcsd.org.

Craik, K.J.W. (1943). *The nature of explanation*. Cambridge, UK: Cambridge Univerisity Press.

Cramer, J. (2005). Company learning about Corporate Social Responsibility. *Business strategy and the environment*. 14(4). 255 -266.

Crooks,M.(2011). Semantikos: Understanding and Cognitive Meaning. Part 1: Two Epistemologies. *Journal of Mind and Behavior*. Vol. 12 (2), Institute of Mind and Behaviour Inc.

De George, R.T. (2000). Business ethics and the challenge of the information age.*Business Ethics Quarterly, 10*(1), 63-72.

Devinney, T.M., Midgley, D.F. &Venaik, S. (2000). The optimal performance of the global firm: Formalizing and extending the integration-responsiveness framework. *Organization Science, 11*(6), 674-695.

Drucker, P.F. (1988). The coming of the new organization. *Harvard Business Review*, 66(1), 45-53.

Du Toit, A.S.A., Van Staden, J.R. & Steyn, D.P. (2011).South Africa's future knowledge workers: A peep into their goals and motivations for innovation. *African Journal of Library and Information Science,* 21(2), 87-97.

Dunphy, D. (2003). Corporate sustainability: Challenge to managerial orthodoxies. *Journal of Australian and New Zealand Academy of Management, 9*(1), 2-11.

Ellis S., Margalit, D. &Segev, E. (2012).Effects of organizational learning mechanisms on organizational performance and shared mental models during planned changed.*Knowledge and Process Management, 19*(2), 91-102.

Erez, M., &Gati, E. (2004). A dynamic, multi-level model of culture: from the micro level of the individual to the macro level of a global culture. *Applied Psychology, 53*(4), 583-598.

Fearis, B. (2005). 'Leadership without borders: Successful strategies from world-class leaders'. *Business Week*, p. 1; McGraw-Hill Companies.

Friedman, B.A. (2007). Globalisation implications for human resource management roles. *Employee Responsibilities and Rights Journal, 19*(3), 157-171. doi: 10.1007/s10672-007-9043-1.

García, M.U. &Vañó, F.L. (2002). Organizational learning in a global market. *Human Systems Management, 21*(3), 169-181.

Ghoshal, S. (2005). Bad management theories are destroying good management practices. *Academy of Management Learning and Education.* 4(1).

Giacalone, R.A. & Thompson, K.R. (2006).Business ethics and social responsibility education: Shifting the worldview. *Academy of Management Learning & Education, 5*(3), 266-277.

Goold, M. & Campbell, A. (2002). *Do you have a well-designed organisation?* Harvard Business Review.

Guo, X. (2013). Living in a global world: Influence of consumer global orientation on attitudes toward global brands from developed versus emerging countries. *Journal of International Marketing, 21*(1), 1-22.

Havenga, W., Mehana V., and Visagie J.C. (2011). Developing a national cadre of effective leadership towards sustainable quality service delivery in South Africa. *African Journal of Business Management, 5*(31), 12271-12282.

Herrinton, M. (2010). *UCT study shows recession has hit SA Entrepreneurship hard.* Retrieved 02-08-2010 from http:www.leader.co.za./pmprintantieleaspx? 5=68 -1&1=2022.

Hofstede, G. (2011). *Cultural Dimensions.* Retrieved from http://www.geert-hofstede.com/hoftede_dimensions.php.

Jackson, T.W. (2006). Customer value exchange. *Journal of Financial Service Marketing, 11*(4), 314-332.

Javidan, M. and Dastmalchian, A.(2009). Managerial implications of the Globe Project: A study of 62 societies.*Asia Pacific Journal of Human Resources*, 47(1)

Kahane, A. (2004). *Solving touch problems: An open way of talking, listening, and creating new realities*. San Francisco, Berea – Koehler Publishers.

Kim, D. (1994). The link between individual and organizational learning. *Sloan Management Review,* 37-50.

Klimoski, R.J. & Mohammed, S. (1994).Team mental model:Construct or metaphor?*Journal of Management*, 20, 403-437.

Lancaster, C.L. & Stillman, D. (2012). *The M-factor: How the millennial generation is rocking the workplace*.New York:HarperCollins.

Landy, F.J. & Conte M.J. (2007). Work in the 21st Century:An introduction to Industrial and Organizational Psychology (2nd ed.). USA: Blackwell Publishers.

Lawler, E.E. & Worley, C.G. (2011). *Management reset: Organizing for sustainable effectiveness*. San Francisco: Jossey-Bass Publishers.

Loughlin, C. & Barling J. (2001). Young workers' work values, attitudes, and behaviours. *Journal of Occupational and Organisational Psychology*, 74(4), 543-558.

Manuel, T. *National Development Plan launch speech by Trevor A Manuel, Minister in the Presidency*: National Planning Commission.https://www.gov.za/national-development-plan-launch-speech-trevor-manuel-minister-presidency-national-planning.

Margalit, D.; Ellis, S. and Sagev, E. (2012). Effects of Organisational Learning Mechanisms on Organisational Performance and Shared Mental Models during Planned Change. *Knowledge and Process Management,* Vol 19(2), 91-102.

Markovic, R.M. (2008).Managing the organizational change and culture in the age of globalisation.*Journal of Business Economics and Management, 9*(1), 3-11.

Marques, J. (2006). A new paradigm of leaders: Macro to micro approach. *Management Services*. Institute of Management Services.

Mathews, J.A. (2006). Dragon multinationals: New players in 21st-century globalisation. *Asia Pacific Journal of Management, 23*(1), 5-27.

Meister, J.C. &Willyerd, K. (2010). *The 2020 Workplace*. New York: HarperCollins Publishers.

Merz, M.A. & Yi, H. (2008). A categorization approach to analysing the global consumer culture debate.*International Marketing Review, 25* (2), 166-82.

Meyer, N.A.T. &Boninelli, I. (2004). *Conversations in leadership – South African perspectives*. South Africa: Knowledge Resources Publishing.

Mukerjee, K. & Singh, K. (2009). CRM: A strategic approach. *ICFAI journal of management research*, 8(2), 65-82.

Mukerjee, K. & Singh, K. (2009). CRM: A strategic approach. ICFAIjournal of management research, 8(2), 65-82.

Nel, C. &Beudeker, N. (2011). *The leadership revolution*(2nd ed.). South Africa:Knowledge Resources Publishing.

Obama, Barack. (2009). *Inaugural address*. Available athttps://obamawhitehouse.archives.gov/blog/2009/01/21/president-barack-obamas-inaugural-address.

OECD. (2017). Enhancing the contributions of SMEsin a globaland digitalised economy.

Parker, B. (2005). Introduction to globalisation & business. London: Sage.

Pillay, P. (2000). South Africa in the 21st century: some key socio-economic challenges. South Africa: Friedrich Ebert Stiftung.

Prahalad, C.K. (2005). *The fortune at the bottom of the pyramid: Eradicating poverty through profits*. Upper Saddle River. NJ: Wharton School Publishing.

Ramaphosa, Cyril. (n.d.). *Address by the President of South Africa to the UN General Assembly*. Available at http://www.thedti.gov.za/UNGA.jsp.

Rich, P. B (Ed.), (1994). The dynamics of change in Southern Africa. New York: St Martins Press.

Rook, L. (2013). Mental models: a robust definition. *The Learning Organisation, 20*(1), 38-47. Bingley, UK: Emerald Group Publishing Limited.

Seidler, M. (2009). *Power Surge: A conduit for enlightened leadership.*Amherst, MA:HRD Press.

Senge, P.M., Kleiner, A., Roberts, C., Ross, R. & Smith, B. (1994). *The fifth discipline fieldbook: Strategies and tools for building a learning organization.* New York: Currency/Doubleday.

Starbuck, W.A. & Milliken, F.J. (1988). Executives' perceptual filters: What they notice and how they make sense. In Hambrick, D.C. (Ed.), *The executive effect: concepts and methods for studying top managers,* pp.35- 650. Greenwich: JAI Press.

Taylor, G.R., &Lynham, A.S.(2013). Systemic leadership for socio-political stewardship.*South African Journal of Business Management, 44*(1), 87-99.

Tetenbaum, T.J. (1998). Shifting paradigms from Newton to Chaos. *Organizational Dynamics, 26*(4), 21-32.

Thomas, T.E. &Lamm, E. (2012). Legitimacy and Organizational Sustainability. *Journal of Business Ethics* 110(2), 191-203. doi: 10.1007/s10551-012-1421-4.

Tom, Peters (1991). Thriving on Chaos: Handbook for a Management Revolution. Harper Collins Publishers, NY 10022.

Tustin, D.H., Ligthelm, A.A., Martins, J.H., & Van Wyk, J de H. (2005). *Marketing research in practice.* Pretoria: Unisa Press.

Van Tonder, C. (2008). *Organization identity as managerial concern.*Retrieved June 2013 from https://ujdigispace.uj.ac.za/handle/10210/5318

Veldsman, T.H. (2002*). Into the people effectiveness arena: Navigating between chaos and order.* Rosebank: Knowledge Resources.

Verwey, A. (2006). Building Leadership Strength. A practical framework for understanding the work, validation and development of leaders and leadership in your business.Unpublished paper.

Verwey, A., Van der Merwe, L. & du Plessis, F. (2012). *Reshaping leadership DNA: A field guide.* South Africa: Knowres Publishing.

Werhane, P.H. (2007). Mental models, moral imagination and system thinkingin the age of globalisation. *Journal of Business Ethics, 78*(3), 463-474.

Wheatley, M.J.(2006). *Leadership and the new science: Discovering order in a chaotic world* (3rd ed.) San Francisco, CA: Berrett-Koehler.

Worden, N. (2007). The making of modern South Africa: Conquest, Apartheid, Democracy (4th ed.). Malden, MA: Blackwell Publishing.

Zadek, S. (2001). *The civil corporation.* London. Earthscan. World Business Council for Sustainable Development.

ENDNOTES

---

[1]Drucker, P.F. (1988). The coming of the new organization. *Harvard Business Review*, 66(1), 45-53.

[2]Taylor, G.R., & Lynham, A.S.(2013). Systemic leadership for socio-political stewardship.*South African Journal of Business Management, 44*(1), 87-99.

[3]Drucker, 'New organization'.

[4]Ibid.

[5]3. Lawler, E.E. & Worley, C.G. (2011). *Management reset: Organizing for sustainable effectiveness*. San Francisco: Jossey-Bass Publishers.

[6]Ibid at 2.

[7]Ibid.

[8]Coetzee, J. (2012). *The social contract with business*. Bloomington, IS: Xlibris Corporation Publishing.

[9] Peters, Tom. (1991). *Thriving on Chaos: Handbook for a Management Revolution*. Harper Collins Publishers, NY 10022.

[10]Tetenbaum, T.J. (1998). Shifting paradigms from Newton to Chaos. *Organizational Dynamics*, 26(4), 21-32.

[11]Marques, J. (2006). A new paradigm of leaders: Macro to micro approach. *Management Services*. Institute of Management Services.

[12]Lawlor & Worley, *Management reset* at 5.

[13]Coetzee, *The social contract with business*.

[14]Dunphy, D. (2003). Corporate sustainability: Challenge to managerial orthodoxies. *Journal of Australian and New Zealand Academy of Management, 9*(1), 2-11.

[15] Ibid.

[16] Crooks, M. (2011), Rook, L. (2013), Barr, P.S., Stimpert, J.L. & Huff, A.S. (1992), Margalit, D., Ellis, S. and Sagev, E. (2012).

[17]Craik, K.J.W. (1943). *The nature of explanation*. Cambridge, UK: Cambridge Univerisity Press.

[18] Ibid.

[19] Kim, D. (1994). The link between individual and organizational learning. *Sloan Management Review*, 37-50; Klimoski, R.J. & Mohammed, S. (1994). Team mental model: Construct or metaphor? *Journal of Management*, 20, 403-437.

[20] Klimoski & Mohammed, Team mental model; Worden, N. (2007). The making of modern South Africa: Conquest, Apartheid, Democracy (4th ed.). Malden, MA: Blackwell Publishing; Parker, B. (2005). Introduction to globalisation & business. London: Sage.

[21]Beinart, W. (2001). *Twentieth century South Africa* (2nd ed.). Oxford: Oxford University Press.

[22]Ibid.

[23] 22. Pillay, P. (2000). *South Africa in the 21st century: some key socio-economic challenges*. South Africa: Friedrich Ebert Stiftung; Herrinton, M. (2010). *UCT study shows recession has hit SA Entrepreneurship hard*. Retrieved 02-08-2010 from http:www.leader.co.za./pm printantiele aspx? 5=68 - 1&1=2022; Starbuck, W.A. & Milliken, F.J. (1988). Executives' perceptual filters: What they notice and how they make sense. In Hambrick, D.C. (Ed.), *The executive effect: concepts and methods for studying top managers*, pp. 35-650. Greenwich: JAI Press.

[24]Prahalad, C.K. (2005). *The fortune at the bottom of the pyramid: Eradicating poverty through profits*. Upper Saddle River. NJ: Wharton School Publishing.

[25]Coetzee, *The social contract with business*;Prahalad, C.K. (2005). *The fortune at the bottom of the pyramid: Eradicating poverty through profits*. Upper Saddle River. NJ: Wharton School Publishing; Meyer, N.A.T. & Boninelli, I. (2004). *Conversations in leadership – South African perspectives*. South Africa: Knowledge Resources Publishing.

[26] Obama, Barack. (2009). *Inaugural address*. Available at https://obamawhitehouse.archives.gov/blog/2009/01/21/president-barack-obamas-inaugural-address.

[27]Coetzee,*The social contract with business*.

[28]Ramaphosa, Cyril. (n.d.). *Address by the President of South Africa to the UN General Assembly*. Available at http://www.thedti.gov.za/UNGA.jsp.

[29]Coetzee, *The social contract with business* at 15.

[30]Prahalad, *The fortune at the bottom of the pyramid*at 243.

[31]Zadek, S. (2001). *The civil corporation*. London. Earthscan. World Business Council for Sustainable Development, page 245.

[32] Manuel, T. *National Development Plan launch speech by Trevor A Manuel, Minister in the Presidency*: National Planning Commission.https://www.gov.za/national-development-plan-launch-speech-trevor-manuel-minister-presidency-national-planning

[33]Havenga, W., Mehana V., and Visagie J.C. (2011). Developing a national cadre of effective leadership towards sustainable quality service delivery in South Africa. *African Journal of Business Management*, 5(31), 12271-12282.

[34]Nel, C. & Beudeker, N. (2011). *The leadership revolution* (2nd ed.). South Africa: Knowledge Resources Publishing.

[35]Ibid.

[36] Fearis, B. (2005). 'Leadership without borders: Successful strategies from world-class leaders'. *Business Week*, p. 1; McGraw-Hill Companies.

[37]Adonis, M. and van Wyk, R. (2012). The influence of Market Orientation, Flexibility and Job Service on Corporate Entrepreneurship. *International Business & Economics Research Journal*, 11 (5).

[38]34. Bhagat, S.R., Segovis, C.J., & Nelson, A.T. (2012). *Work stress and coping in the era of globalisation*. New York: Routledge Taylor and Francis Group.

[39]Cohen, E. (2008). Welcome to the new global frontier. *T AND D*, 62(2),www.wbcsd.org.

[40]OECD. (2017). *Enhancing the contributions of SMEs in a global and digitalised economy*, p8.

[41]Lancaster, C.L. & Stillman, D. (2012). *The M-factor: How the millennial generation is rocking the workplace*. New York: HarperCollins.

[42]OECD. *Enhancing the contributions of SMEs*.

[43] Mukerjee & Singh. CRM: A strategic approach; 38. Bennis, W. and Mische, M. (1995). *The 21st century organisation: Re-inventing through re-engineering*. San Diego: Pfeiffer & Co.; Jackson, T.W. (2006). Customer value exchange. *Journal of Financial Service Marketing*, 11(4), 314-332; Guo, X. (2013). Living in a global world: Influence of consumer global orientation on attitudes toward global brands from developed versus emerging countries. *Journal of International Marketing*, 21(1), 1-22; Merz, M.A. & Yi, H. (2008). A categorization approach to analysing the global consumer culture debate. *International Marketing Review*, 25 (2), 166-82.

[44]Cohen, 'Welcome to the new global frontier' at 54.

[45]Ibid.

[46]Loughlin, C. & Barling J. (2001). Young workers' work values, attitudes, and behaviours. *Journal of Occupational and Organisational Psychology*, 74(4), 543-558.

[47]Lancaster & Stillman. *The M-factor*at 86.

[48]Meister, J.C. & Willyerd, K. (2010). *The 2020 Workplace*. New York: HarperCollins Publishers, p 103.

[49]Bhagat& Segovis, *Work stress* at 40.

[50]Meister & Willyerd, *The 2020 Workplace*.

[51]Friedman, B.A. (2007). Globalisation implications for human resource management roles. *Employee Responsibilities and Rights Journal*, 19(3), 157-171. doi: 10.1007/s10672-007-9043-1.

[52]Nel & Beudeker, *The leadership revolution*at 40.

[53]Ibid at 7.

[54]Nordstrom quoted in Nel & Beudeker, *The leadership revolution* at 7.

[55] Baskin, J. (2006). *Value, values and sustainability: Corporate responsibility in emerging market companies*. Available at http://ssm.com/abstract=1094573; Cho, C.H., Meyer, D.M. & Roberts, R.W. (2006). Corporate political strategy: An examination of the relation between political expenditures, environmental performance and environmental disclosure. *Journal of Business Ethics*, 67(2), 139-154; Giacalone, R.A. & Thompson, K.R. (2006). Business ethics and social responsibility education: Shifting the worldview. *Academy of Management Learning & Education*, 5(3), 266-277; Cramer, J. (2005). Company learning about Corporate Social Responsibility. *Business strategy and the environment*. 14(4). 255 -266.

[56]Thomas, T.E. & Lamm, E. (2012). Legitimacy and Organizational Sustainability. *Journal of Business Ethics* 110(2), 191-203. doi: 10.1007/s10551-012-1421-4.

[57]Baskin, *Value, values and sustainability*.

[58] Thomas, T.E. & Lamm, E. (2012). Legitimacy and Organizational Sustainability. *Journal of Business Ethics* 110(2), 191-203. doi: 10.1007/s10551-012-1421-4; Ajzen, I. (2001). Nature and operaton of attitudes. Annual Review of Psychology, 52, 27-58.

[59]Thomas & Lamm, 'Legitimacy and Organizational Sustainability'.

[60]Markovic, R.M. (2008). Managing the organizational change and culture in the age of globalisation. *Journal of Business Economics and Management*, 9(1), 3-11.

[61] Ellis S., Margalit, D. & Segev, E. (2012). Effects of organizational learning mechanisms on organizational performance and shared mental models during planned changed. *Knowledge and Process Management*, 19(2), 91-102; Friedman, B.A. (2007). Globalisation implications for human resource management roles. *Employee Responsibilities and Rights Journal*, 19(3), 157-171. doi: 10.1007/s10672-007-9043-1; García, M.U. & Vañó, F.L. (2002). Organizational learning in a global market. *Human Systems Management*, 21(3), 169-181; De George, R.T. (2000). Business ethics and the challenge of the information age. Business Ethics Quarterly, 10(1), 63-72.

[62]Werhane, P.H. (2007). Mental models, moral imagination and system thinking in the age of globalisation. *Journal of Business Ethics*, 78(3), 463-474.

[63]Wheatley, M.J. (2006). *Leadership and the new science: Discovering order in a chaotic world* (3rd ed.) San Francisco, CA: Berrett-Koehler, p 4.

[64]Ibid at 11.

[65]Goold, M. & Campbell, A. (2002). *Do you have a well-designed organisation?* Harvard Business Review.

[66]Wheatley, *Leadership and the new science* at 104.

[67]Devinney, T.M., Midgley, D.F. & Venaik, S. (2000). The optimal performance of the global firm: Formalizing and extending the integration-responsiveness framework. *Organization Science*, 11(6), 674-695.

[68]Goold & Campbell, *Do you have a well-designed organisation?*

[69]Ghoshal, S. (2005). Bad management theories are destroying good management practices. *Academy of Management Learning and Education*. 4(1).

[70]Markovic, 'Managing the organizational change and culture'; Goold & Campbell, *Do you have a well-designed organisation?*; Ghoshal, 'Bad management theories'.

[71]Javidan, M. and Dastmalchian, A. (2009). Managerial implications of the Globe Project: A study of 62 societies.*Asia Pacific Journal of Human Resources, 47(1)*.

[72]Hofstede, G. (2011). *Cultural Dimensions.* Retrieved from http://www.geert-hofstede.com/hoftede_dimensions.php.

[73]Ghoshal, 'Bad management theories' at 38.

[74]Meyer, & Boninelli, *Conversations in leadership.*

[75] Manuel, T. *National Development Plan launch speech.*

[76]Meyer, & Boninelli, *Conversations in leadership.*

[77]Blanchard, K. (1994). *The one-minute manager.* London: Harper Collins.

[78]Blake, R. & Mouton, J. (1985). *The Managerial Grid III: The Key to Leadership Excellence.* Houston: Gulf Publishing Co.

[79]Verwey, A., Van der Merwe, L. & du Plessis, F. (2012). *Reshaping leadership DNA: A field guide.* South Africa: Knowres Publishing.

[80]Drucker, 'The coming of the new organization'; Thomas & Lamm, 'Legitimacy and Organizational Sustainability'; Werhane, 'Mental models, moral imagination and system thinking'; Benvenista, G. (1994). *The twenty-first century organisation: Analyzing current trends, imagining the future.* San Francisco, CA: Jossey-Bass Publishers.

[81]Werhane, 'Mental models, moral imagination and system thinking' at 16.

[82]Taylor, & Lynham, 'Systemic leadership for socio-political stewardship'; Nel & Beudeker, 'The leadership revolution'; Werhane, 'Mental models, moral imagination and system thinking'; Seidler, M. (2009). *Power Surge: A conduit for enlightened leadership.* Amherst, MA: HRD Press.

[83]Zadek, S. (2001). *The civil corporation.* London. Earthscan. World Business Council for Sustainable Development.

[84]Veldsman, T.H. (2002). *Into the people effectiveness arena: Navigating between chaos and order.* Rosebank: Knowledge Resources.

[85]Nel & Beudeker, *The leadership revolution.*

[86]Ibid at 50.

[87]Verwey, Van der Merwe, & du Plessis, *Reshaping leadership DNA.*

[88]Ghoshal, S. (2005). Bad management theories are destroying good management practices. *Academy of Management Learning and Education.* 4(1).